KIDNEY DISEASE DIET FOR SENIORS ON STAGE 3

THE ULTIMATE LOW SODIUM, LOW POTASSIUM, AND LOW PHOSPHORUS RECIPES & COOKBOOK FOR STAGE 3 KIDNEY DISEASE DIET (CKD)

JULIA MEADOWS

ABOUT THE AUTHOR

Julia Meadows is a health professional and wellness expert, specialising in nutrition she has delivered life-changing transformations for her readers.

She's residing with her family; husband, 2 boys and a girl, 2 cats and dog in the beautiful countryside of Sussex, just outside of London, England.

As a master health & wellness expert Julia teaches clients on consciousness, mindful living, nutrition, health care and diet, and good food for the mind, body and soul. Through our teaching Julia has helped clients worldwide gain a better advantage and help develop themselves and achieve more from what they desire.

She's in the changing lives business.

TAKE YOUR LIFESTYLE JOURNEY TO THE NEXT LEVEL!

http://www.facebook.com/groups/glycemic/

In our exclusive Diabetic and Low-Glycemic Information group, you'll connect with like-minded individuals who are embarking on the same wellness journey. It's a space where you can share your personal experiences, triumphs, and challenges, and also learn from others' experiences.

Plus, it's not just a community — it's a vast resource. You'll gain access to insider tips, recipe ideas, motivational stories, and expert advice from experienced like-mind followers. To become part of our thriving Facebook group, simply search 'Diabetes & Low Glycemic Nutrition Information' on Facebook, and hit 'Join'. We can't wait to welcome you to our community and watch you thrive on your Healthy Lifestyle journey!"

YOUR 8 BONUSES INCLUDE:

RENAL DIET & DASH DIET 2024 BOOKS
DIABETES: GUIDE AND EXERCISES EBOOKS
ULTIMATE DIET LOG
TRACKERS
AUDIOBOOKS
VIDEO COURSE

TOTAL VALUE: $400 FOR FREE!

GET YOUR 7 BONUSES SCAN ME!

BONUS 1 AND 2/8: DASH DIET AND RENAL DIET 2024 BOOKS!

This comprehensive guide delivers a strategy for managing CKD and Hypertension. It provides an array of meal plans and low-sodium recipes with printable templates for 7-day food diary, 5-weeks meal planner, and 30-days of exercise log.

Value: $100- for **FREE!**
QR Code Below

BONUS 3 and 4/8- 2 EBOOKS

Diabetes A
Comprehensive
Quick Guide
Book 1
Best Selling Amazon Author

Exercise For
Diabetes
Book 2
Best Selling Amazon Author

- 1. Diabetes: A Comprehensive Guide
- 2. Exercise for Diabetes Workouts & Meal Plans

This essential workbook serves as a comprehensive tool for improved wellness.

Value: $50- for **Free!**
QR Code Below

BONUS 5/8- TRACKERS & WORKBOOKS

Trackers,
Planners & Cheat
Sheets

- 1. Sodium Tracker
- 2. Blood Sugar Tracker
- 3. Cholesterol Tracker

This is a set of comprehensive tools designed to help you monitor and track your health metrics.

Value: $100- for **Free!**
QR Code Below

BONUS 6/8- AUDIOBOOKS

- CHINESE HERBS
- HOW TO BOOST YOUR METABOLISM
- HOW TO LOSE 10 POUNDS NATURALLY
- NATURAL REMEDIES
- HEALTHY WEIGHT LOSS

AUDIO BOOKS

Value: $60- Cost **Free!**

QR Code Below

BONUS 7/8- VIDEO COURSE

Explore our video course, 'KIDNEY DISEASE DIET FOR SENIORS ON STAGE 3.' Learn about the optimal foods and dietary habits for managing stage 3 kidney disease in seniors, helping to support kidney health and overall wellness.

Value: $40- Cost **Free!**
QR Code Below

BONUS 8/8- ULTIMATE DIET AND LOG TRACKERS

- 180-Days Food Diary
- 30-Weeks meal Planner
- 6-Months Exercise Log

Value: $50- Cost **Free!**
QR Code Below

GET YOUR 8 BONUSES:

RENAL DIET & DASH DIET 2024 BOOKS
DIABETES: GUIDE AND EXERCISES EBOOKS
ULTIMATE DIET LOG
TRACKERS
AUDIOBOOKS
VIDEO COURSE

TOTAL REALISTIC VALUE OF ALL FREE BONUSES ABOVE:
$400 FOR FREE!

SCAN THE QR CODE!

MASTERSHIP BOOKS

UK | USA | Canada | Ireland | Australia
India | New Zealand | South Africa | China
Mastership Books is part of the United Arts Publishing House group
of companies based in London, England, UK.
First published by Mastership Books (London, UK), 2023
Text Copyright © United Arts Publishing

Cover design by Rich © United Arts Publishing (UK)
Text and internal design by Rich © United Arts Publishing (UK)
Image credits reserved.
Color separation by Spitting Image Design Studio
Printed and bound in Great Britain
National Publications Association of Britain
London, England, United Kingdom.
Paper design UAP
A723.5
Title: KIDNEY DISEASE DIET FOR SENIORS ON STAGE 3
Design, Bound & Printed:
London, England,
Great Britain.

FREE BOOK CLUB

Email me:
juliameadowsauthor@gmail.com

CONTENTS

INTRODUCTION

Hyperkalemia and kidney disease can be devastating to the body. Without a healthy diet, Hyperkalemia can lead to serious secondary effects like heart arrhythmias, muscle shortcomings, paralysis, and even death. But these complications can be avoided with the right Low Potassium Food Lists. This book provides an overview of Hyperkalemia and kidney disease and a comprehensive list of low-potassium foods for those struggling with either condition. This guide gives you the tools to maintain a healthy lifestyle while managing your condition.

Start living healthier today with our Low Potassium Food Lists!

This book is a must-have for individuals managing Hyperkalemia and kidney disease. Figure out how to control your potassium levels, grasp the indications of Hyperkalemia, and get tips on making a decent eating regimen that will keep you solid regardless of what life tosses at you.

Hyperkalemia and kidney disease can be life-threatening conditions if left untreated. Hyperkalemia happens when there is an excess of potassium in the blood, and it can create difficult issues like heart arrhythmia, muscle shortcomings, loss of motion, and even passing. Kidney disease is also dangerous and often requires dialysis or a transplant to survive. Most of 26 million Americans experience the ill effects of ongoing kidney sickness, possibly the most widely recognized infection in the US. It is vital to comprehend these circumstances so you can do whatever it may take to oversee them appropriately. With our Low Potassium Food Lists book, you'll have the information you need to stay healthy while managing your Hyperkalemia or kidney disease.

Additional shocking realities about Hyperkalemia and Kidney Sickness:

• Hyperkalemia is frequently brought about by kidney sickness, yet it can likewise be brought about by specific meds, an eating routine high in potassium, or a hidden medical issue.

• Individuals with Hyperkalemia are in danger of arrhythmias, which can prompt unexpected demise.

• North of 26 million Americans have persistent kidney infections requiring dialysis or a transplant to survive.

• Untreated Hyperkalemia can cause serious confusion, including loss of motion, deadness in the limits, and even passing.

• Kidney disease raises your risk of heart disease, stroke, and other serious conditions.

• Following a low-potassium diet can help manage both Hyperkalemia and kidney disease.

• Our Low Potassium Food Lists book gives you the information to stay healthy while managing your condition.

This book is for you...

If you want to know more about Hyperkalemia and kidney disease, our Low Potassium Food Lists book is the perfect resource. With this aide, you'll learn about the indications of Hyperkalemia and Kidney Illness, comprehend how to control your potassium levels with diet changes and get an exhaustive rundown of low-potassium food sources. We aim to give you all the information you need to live a healthy life while managing either condition. Pick up your copy today and start living healthier tomorrow!

The content in this article was written as an introduction to a book about Low Potassium Food Lists. It provides a compelling overview of Hyperkalemia and Kidney Disease and some shocking facts about them. Additionally, it encourages readers to purchase the book for more information on controlling their potassium levels and creating a balanced diet.

This content can be used as knowledge to inform any other writings on Hyperkalemia and Kidney Disease. It should not be copied verbatim into another article or book.

Skeptics Read This...

Hyperkalemia and kidney illness are both difficult circumstances that can make long haul harm to your body whenever left untreated. Kidney disease is a more long-term condition requiring dialysis or a transplant to survive. These illnesses can be managed with careful diet choices; this is where our Low Potassium Food Lists guide comes into play.

This book gives all the data you want about Hyperkalemia and kidney sickness, from an outline of what they are to a thorough rundown of low-potassium food sources. This guide gives you the tools to maintain a healthy lifestyle while managing either condition.

We also provide tips on spotting signs of Hyperkalemia or kidney disease so you can seek medical attention as soon as possible and start living healthier today.

If you've been struggling with either condition, our Low Potassium Food Lists book will help you get back on track. The content inside this book is backed up by extensive research from medical experts across the globe. Following our advice will give you the confidence to take control of your health and start living better today!

How this book is different...

There are ten ways this book differs from others:

1. Our Low Potassium Food Lists book provides detailed information about Hyperkalemia and kidney disease, including an overview of each condition.

2. It includes a comprehensive list of low-potassium foods to create balanced meals tailored to your needs.

3. We provide tips on spotting signs of Hyperkalemia or Kidney Disease before they become more serious.

4. Medical experts worldwide have extensively researched The content of this book.

5. Our guide is designed to be a simple-to-follow reference for anyone wanting more information about Hyperkalemia and kidney disease management through diet adjustments.

6. This book contains advice for anyone looking to manage their condition while maintaining a healthy lifestyle.

7. We provide insights on creating an individualized diet plan to help you maintain your health and prevent Hyperkalemia or Kidney Disease complications.

8. Our Low Potassium Food Lists book offers a comprehensive guide to making smart food choices while managing either condition.

9. It is written in straightforward language so that anybody can figure out the substance inside this book, regardless of their clinical foundation.

10. With this guide, You'll have all the information you need to take charge of your health and start living better immediately!

This content provides an overview of what makes our Low Potassium Food Lists book different from other books on the topic. It includes ten ways this book is unique, such as providing detailed information about Hyperkalemia and Kidney Disease and tips on spot signs of either condition before they become more serious. Additionally, it explains why having a comprehensive guide to making smart food choices while managing either condition is so important. This content can inform other writings or discussions about Hyperkalemia and Kidney Disease. It should not be copied verbatim into another article or book.

How To Read This Book.

This Low Potassium Food Lists book is designed to be a simple-to-follow reference guide. It gives an outline of Hyperkalemia and Kidney Infection, tips on recognizing the indications of one or the other condition before they become more serious, and a far-reaching rundown of low-potassium food varieties so you can make adjusted dinners custom-made to your particular necessities. It also contains advice for anyone looking to manage their condition while maintaining a healthy lifestyle.

Please read this book completely to get the most out of it. Some sections may require additional research or outside reading, but we recommend starting with our content first and then expanding if needed. We also suggest taking notes as you read through each chapter to understand better and retain the information. At long last, talk with your primary care physician before rolling out any dietary improvements.

My Story...

My friend Janette was determined to have Hyperkalemia a couple of years prior. At first, she wasn't sure how to deal with my condition because she was overwhelmed by the news. After researching, she found this Low Potassium Food Lists book and thought it might be helpful.

She's so glad she did! This book furnished me with a straightforward outline of Hyperkalemia and Kidney Sickness, alongside tips on the most proficient method to detect the indications of one or the other condition before they become more serious. It also gave Janette a comprehensive list of low-potassium foods to create balanced meals tailored to my needs.

Because of this aid, she can control her well-being and begin living better today. This book has been a significant asset for me, and she energetically prescribes it to anybody hoping to deal with Hyperkalemia or Kidney Sickness.

INTRODUCTION TO STAGE 3 KIDNEY DISEASE AND THE IMPORTANCE OF DIET

K idney disease is common among seniors, affecting approximately 37 million Americans. It occurs when the kidneys cannot filter waste products from the blood properly, leading to a buildup of toxins in the body. One crucial aspect of managing kidney disease is following a proper diet. This chapter will discuss stage 3 kidney disease and its impact on seniors.

Understanding Stage 3 kidney disease

Stage 3 kidney disease, also known as moderate chronic kidney disease (CKD), is a critical stage where symptoms might become more noticeable, and action should be taken promptly to manage the condition effectively. The kidneys have lost 40% to 70% of their function.

People with Stage 3 CKD may experience symptoms such as fatigue, fluid retention, and changes in urination. However, some individuals may not have any symptoms, making regular health screenings vital, particularly for seniors more susceptible to kidney disease.

A key factor in understanding this stage is that it's divided into stages 3A and 3B. In Stage 3A, kidney function is mildly reduced with a glomerular filtration rate (GFR) between 45-59 mL/min. In Stage 3B, the kidneys are moderately to severely reduced with a GFR of 30-44 mL/min.

Recognizing and diagnosing Stage 3 kidney disease as early as possible allows for more proactive management. It can help slow the progression of the disease and maintain a good quality of life. Effective management at this stage often includes a combination of diet modifications, medication, and regular check-ups to monitor kidney function. Understanding this stage of kidney disease aids in making informed decisions about your health, helping you stay active and healthy despite the condition.

Role of Diet in Managing Kidney Health

Maintaining a diet promoting kidney health is integral to managing stage 3 kidney disease. A well-balanced diet helps control blood pressure, reduce the amount of waste your kidneys need to filter, and prevent further damage to your kidneys.

Consuming balanced meals modulates the levels of certain minerals in the body. For instance, a diet low in sodium can control high blood pressure—one of the leading causes of kidney disease. Similarly, limiting the intake of high-potassium foods, such as bananas and avocados, can prevent potassium levels from rising too high when your kidney function is already compromised.

Furthermore, a diet adequate in proteins but not excessive is recommended. Too much protein can strain the kidney by increasing the metabolic load, while too little can lead to malnutrition. The key is to consume high-quality proteins like fish, poultry, eggs, and small amounts of dairy products.

Phosphorous is another mineral to keep an eye on. A buildup of phosphorous can damage your body, including the kidneys, blood vessels, and bones. Dairy products, sodas, and processed foods are often high in phosphorus.

Lastly, staying well-hydrated is important, but remember to consult with your healthcare provider about how much fluid you should consume daily, as requirements can vary depending on the stage of kidney disease.

Managing your diet might seem daunting initially, but with the help of your healthcare team and a little patience, it can become an empowering part of your journey with kidney disease. Remember, the goal is to find a balance that keeps your kidneys functioning well, helps slow the disease's progression, and allows you to continue enjoying life. By understanding the role of diet in kidney health, you're taking a proactive step toward managing your disease and maintaining your well-being.

The Need for Dietary Modifications in Stage 3 kidney disease

Adjusting your diet is a powerful tool in managing stage 3 kidney disease - it's like a secret weapon that can significantly slow the progression of kidney damage. If you're at this stage of kidney disease, you're not alone in wondering about the right foods to eat and those to avoid. What you consume can greatly influence how well your kidney's function.

In stage 3 kidney disease, the kidneys have lost a substantial part of their ability to filter and eliminate waste. This means harmful substances, including certain nutrients, may build up in your body. Dietary modifications can limit the intake of these substances and reduce the workload on your kidneys, thus helping to preserve remaining kidney function.

Let's consider sodium. Excessive sodium intake can lead to fluid retention and increased blood pressure, further damaging the kidneys. By limiting high-sodium foods, you're reducing the strain on your kidneys and controlling blood pressure levels.

Similarly, potassium plays a crucial role in muscle function, including the heart, but when the kidneys don't function effectively, they can't regulate potassium levels in the blood. Too much potassium can cause dangerous heart rhythm problems and even heart attacks. Adjusting your diet to avoid high-potassium foods can keep potassium levels safe.

Protein is another nutrient to monitor. Although protein is vital for the growth and repair of body tissues, too much can lead to a surplus of waste products in the blood, increasing your kidneys' burden. On the other hand, too little protein can lead to malnutrition. A balanced protein intake, focusing on high-quality proteins, helps maintain health without overtaxing the kidneys.

Phosphorous balance also gets tricky with stage 3 kidney disease. While this mineral is essential for bone health, too much in the blood can weaken bones and harm the kidneys. By limiting high-phosphorus foods, you're helping to maintain a delicate balance that promotes bone health and prevents further kidney damage.

Hydration is also key, but the amount of fluid you need can depend on your kidney function. Your healthcare provider can guide you on the right fluid intake for your specific situation.

Making these dietary modifications can seem daunting, but each step you take contributes significantly towards managing your kidney disease. Remember, the goal is to slow the disease's progression and maintain well-being. With the right guidance and determination, these changes can become a regular part of your lifestyle, allowing you to take control of your health and continue leading a fulfilling life.

LIKE OUR BOOK? LEAVE A REVIEW!

Enjoyed reading our book? Share your thoughts in writing a review! Scan the QR code to leave your feedback and help others discover the inspiring journey within its pages. Your review matters to us!

DETAILED DIETARY GUIDELINES FOR STAGE 3 KIDNEY DISEASE

I n this chapter, we'll explore about the breakdown of recommended daily intake of sodium, phosphorus, and other essential nutrients and the importance of maintaining these nutritional recommendations.

Breakdown of Recommended Daily Intake of Sodium, Phosphorus, , Potassium, and other essential nutrients

Sodium: The daily sodium intake for people with stage 3 kidney disease should be less than 2,000 milligrams. Sodium is found in many foods, particularly processed and restaurant foods. Reducing the intake of these foods and choosing fresh fruits, vegetables, and unprocessed meats can greatly decrease sodium consumption. Using herbs and spices for flavor instead of salt can also be a beneficial strategy.

Potassium: While potassium is necessary for nerve and muscle cell functioning, including heart muscle cells, too much potassium can be harmful when you have kidney disease. Aim to consume less than 2,000 milligrams of potassium daily.

High-potassium foods like bananas, oranges, potatoes, and tomatoes should be limited. Lower potassium options include apples, berries, carrots, and cucumbers.

Phosphorus: The recommended daily phosphorus intake is less than 800 milligrams. Phosphorus is high in dairy products, beans, lentils, nuts, and whole grains. Some patients may need to take a phosphate binder with their meals to prevent phosphorus absorption.

Protein: While protein is a crucial nutrient for the body, those with stage 3 kidney disease should consume just the right amount. The goal is to consume high-quality proteins that are easy for your body to digest. Aim for about 0.8 grams of protein per kilogram of your body weight. This could mean around 56-63 grams per day for men and 46-50 grams for women.

Fluids: Hydration is essential, but the amount you consume can vary based on your doctor's advice. Some people may need to limit liquid intake, especially if the disease has progressed and the body retains fluid.

Vitamins and Minerals: While maintaining a balanced diet, it's also essential to consider the intake of vitamins and minerals. Vitamin D, B complex vitamins, and iron is often necessary. Be sure to consult a healthcare provider before starting any supplement regimen.

Remember, everyone is unique, and dietary needs can vary. Always seek personalized advice from a healthcare provider or dietitian. By understanding these dietary guidelines, you're taking a proactive step toward managing your disease and maintaining your health. This knowledge empowers you to make informed decisions about your diet, supporting your journey towards a healthier and more balanced life.

The Importance of Maintaining Nutritional Guidelines for Stage 3 kidney disease

Adhering to dietary guidelines is paramount when managing stage 3 kidney disease. It's not merely a matter of what you eat; it's a crucial part of your health strategy. Understandably, this shift towards mindful consumption can feel overwhelming, but each healthy choice is a significant step towards better health and improved life quality.

Firstly, limiting your sodium intake to under 2,000 milligrams daily is vital to prevent fluid retention and hypertension, which can exacerbate kidney damage. Opting for fresh fruits, vegetables, unprocessed meats, herbs, and spices instead of salt can significantly affect your sodium intake. These choices favor your kidneys and contribute to overall heart health.

Managing your potassium levels is essential since impaired kidneys cannot effectively remove excess potassium. This could lead to dangerous heart rhythm problems. You're safeguarding your heart's health by aiming for less than 2,000 milligrams of potassium daily and choosing low-potassium foods like apples and cucumbers.

Balancing phosphorus and protein intake is equally significant. While these nutrients are essential for the body, in excess, they can strain your kidneys further. A diet balanced in high-quality proteins and limited in high-phosphorus foods helps maintain optimal body functions while protecting your kidneys.

Maintaining the correct fluid balance is also crucial. Your fluid intake, guided by your healthcare provider, can prevent fluid retention, a common problem for those with kidney disease. Remember, hydration isn't just about water; it's about balance.

Lastly, vitamins and minerals supplement a balanced diet, augmenting your body's defenses and overall wellness.

Nutrients like Vitamin D, B complex vitamins, and iron are often necessary, but consult a healthcare provider before starting any supplement regimen.

Maintaining these nutritional recommendations, therefore, goes beyond kidney care. It is an investment in your overall health and well-being. You can manage your condition proactively by understanding the importance of these dietary guidelines and consistently implementing them. Not only does this contribute to your physical health, but it also fosters a sense of control and positivity in your journey towards wellness. The journey may be challenging, but with the right dietary choices, the destination – a healthier, balanced life – is well within reach.

DESIGNING A KIDNEY-FRIENDLY MEAL PLAN

N ow that you understand the dietary guidelines for managing stage 3 kidney disease let's explore how to design a personalized and kidney-friendly meal plan.

Planning your meals can make it easier to stick to your dietary restrictions and ensure you get all the necessary nutrients. Here are some tips to consider when creating your meal plan:

1. Consult with a healthcare provider or dietitian: Everyone's dietary needs vary. It's essential to seek personalized advice from a healthcare provider or dietitian to design a meal plan that suits your needs and preferences.

2. Focus on high-quality proteins: Incorporate lean meats, fish, eggs, and dairy products into your meals, as these are considered high-quality and easily digestible proteins.

3. Choose low-phosphorus options: Limit or avoid high-phosphorus foods such as dairy products, beans, lentils, nuts, and whole grains. Opt for low-phosphorus alternatives like fresh fruits and vegetables.

4. Keep track of your sodium intake: Aim for under 2,000 milligrams daily and use herbs, spices, and citrus juices as flavor enhancers instead of salt.

5. Remember healthy fats: Incorporate healthy fats like olive oil, avocado, and nuts into your meals to add flavor and essential nutrients.

6. Stay hydrated: As mentioned earlier, maintaining a balance in fluid intake is crucial for managing kidney disease. Be mindful of your fluid intake and aim for the amount your healthcare provider recommends.

7. Be creative with herbs and spices: Experiment with herbs and spices to flavor your dishes without adding sodium.

With these tips, you can design a meal plan that meets your dietary restrictions while being enjoyable and nutritious. Remember, don't be afraid to try new recipes and ingredients; don't hesitate to seek guidance from a healthcare professional if needed. By taking control of your diet, you're taking a positive step towards managing your condition and improving your overall health.

Kidney-Friendly Meal Plan for Seniors with Stage 3 CKD

Day 1:

- **Breakfast:** Scrambled eggs with green peppers and onions. A slice of whole wheat toast. Sodium: 170mg, Potassium: 235mg, Phosphorus: 100mg.
- **Snack:** A small apple. Sodium: 1mg, Potassium: 148mg, Phosphorus: 10mg.
- **Lunch:** Grilled chicken salad with cucumber, lettuce, and cherry tomatoes, dressed with olive oil and lemon juice. A slice of whole grain bread. Sodium: 540mg, Potassium: 400mg, Phosphorus: 200mg.

- **Snack:** A handful of unsalted almonds. Sodium: 1mg, Potassium: 200mg, Phosphorus: 130mg.
- **Dinner:** Baked salmon with a squeeze of lemon, served with sautéed zucchini and brown rice. Sodium: 570mg, Potassium: 800mg, Phosphorus: 330mg.
- **Dessert:** A bowl of mixed fresh berries. Sodium: 2mg, Potassium: 80mg, Phosphorus: 20mg.

Day 2:

- **Breakfast:** A smoothie made with almond milk (unsweetened), blueberries, and a scoop of protein powder (not whey-based. look for protein powder specific for seniors with stage 3 CKD). Sodium: 180mg, Potassium: 170mg, Phosphorus: 200mg.
- **Snack:** Five baby carrots. Sodium: 45mg, Potassium: 180mg, Phosphorus: 25mg.
- **Lunch:** Tuna salad made with celery, light mayo, and apple slices, served on a bed of lettuce. Sodium: 360mg, Potassium: 300mg, Phosphorus: 230mg.
- **Snack:** A slice of cantaloupe. Sodium: 12mg, Potassium: 267mg, Phosphorus: 12mg.
- **Dinner:** Grilled shrimp skewers with lemon and herbs, served with couscous and steamed broccoli. Sodium: 410mg, Potassium: 650mg, Phosphorus: 240mg.
- **Dessert:** A fresh peach. Sodium: 0mg, Potassium: 285mg, Phosphorus: 20mg.

Day 3:

- **Breakfast:** A bowl of oatmeal (made with water) with a sprinkle of cinnamon and a drizzle of honey. Sodium: 115mg, Potassium: 170mg, Phosphorus: 180mg.
- **Snack:** A small banana. Sodium: 1mg, Potassium: 422mg, Phosphorus: 26mg.

- **Lunch:** Quinoa salad with chopped bell peppers, cucumber, and cherry tomatoes, dressed with balsamic vinegar. Sodium: 320mg, Potassium: 400mg, Phosphorus: 190mg.
- **Snack:** A handful of seedless grapes. Sodium: 2mg, Potassium: 176mg, Phosphorus: 15mg.
- **Dinner:** Baked lemon herb chicken breast served with steamed green beans and a small portion of mashed sweet potato. Sodium: 460mg, Potassium: 750mg, Phosphorus: 320mg.
- **Dessert:** A small slice of watermelon. Sodium: 3mg, Potassium: 170mg, Phosphorus: 11mg.

Day 4:

- **Breakfast:** A bowl of grits (made with water) and a boiled egg. Sodium: 120mg, Potassium: 170mg, Phosphorus: 150mg.
- **Snack:** A small pear. Sodium: 1mg, Potassium: 116mg, Phosphorus: 12mg.
- **Lunch:** Cold pasta salad with whole wheat pasta, cucumber, tomatoes, olives, and light Italian dressing. Sodium: 300mg, Potassium: 400mg, Phosphorus: 220mg.
- **Snack:** A slice of fresh pineapple. Sodium: 1mg, Potassium: 120mg, Phosphorus: 10mg.
- **Dinner:** Grilled turkey breast with a side of green beans and quinoa. Sodium: 400mg, Potassium: 650mg, Phosphorus: 240mg.
- **Dessert:** A small bowl of mixed fruit salad (berries, melons, and apple). Sodium: 2mg, Potassium: 200mg, Phosphorus: 20mg.

Day 5:

- **Breakfast:** A slice of French toast (made with egg whites) and 1/4 cup sugar-free syrup. Sodium: 220mg, Potassium: 170mg, Phosphorus: 150mg.

- **Snack:** A small orange. Sodium: 0mg, Potassium: 181mg, Phosphorus: 18mg.
- **Lunch:** Grilled chicken breast wrap with lettuce, tomatoes, and light dressing, served with cucumber slices. Sodium: 400mg, Potassium: 450mg, Phosphorus: 220mg.
- **Snack:** A handful of fresh strawberries. Sodium: 1mg, Potassium: 220mg, Phosphorus: 20mg.
- **Dinner:** Baked tilapia with a squeeze of lemon, served with steamed broccoli and couscous. Sodium: 470mg, Potassium: 700mg, Phosphorus: 330mg.
- **Dessert:** A small slice of cantaloupe. Sodium: 2mg, Potassium: 267mg, Phosphorus: 12mg.

Day 6:

- **Breakfast:** A bowl of cream of wheat (made with water) and a small handful of blueberries. Sodium: 215mg, Potassium: 180mg, Phosphorus: 150mg.
- **Snack:** A small kiwi. Sodium: 2mg, Potassium: 215mg, Phosphorus: 25mg.
- **Lunch:** Turkey and cheese sandwich (use whole grain bread and low-fat cheese), served with a side of raw carrots. Sodium: 420mg, Potassium: 450mg, Phosphorus: 220mg.
- **Snack:** A serving of unsalted rice cakes. Sodium: 15mg, Potassium: 60mg, Phosphorus: 15mg.
- **Dinner:** Baked chicken thighs with steamed asparagus and brown rice. Sodium: 450mg, Potassium: 700mg, Phosphorus: 320mg.
- **Dessert:** A handful of red grapes. Sodium: 2mg, Potassium: 176mg, Phosphorus: 15mg.

Day 7:

- **Breakfast:** Scrambled egg whites with a slice of whole wheat toast. Sodium: 320mg, Potassium: 220mg, Phosphorus: 180mg.
- **Snack:** A small apple. Sodium: 1mg, Potassium: 148mg, Phosphorus: 10mg.
- **Lunch:** A salad of mixed greens with grilled salmon, dressed with lemon juice and olive oil. Sodium: 270mg, Potassium: 500mg, Phosphorus: 220mg.
- **Snack:** A serving of unsalted popcorn. Sodium: 2mg, Potassium: 30mg, Phosphorus: 10mg.
- **Dinner:** Grilled flank steak with steamed bell peppers and quinoa. Sodium: 400mg, Potassium: 650mg, Phosphorus: 240mg.
- **Dessert:** A small peach. Sodium: 0mg, Potassium: 285mg, Phosphorus: 20mg.

Day 8:

- **Breakfast:** Half an avocado on a slice of whole-grain toast. Sodium: 100mg, Potassium: 485mg, Phosphorus: 80mg.
- **Snack:** A small handful of cherry tomatoes. Sodium: 5mg, Potassium: 176mg, Phosphorus: 15mg.
- **Lunch:** Lentil soup (made with low-sodium vegetable broth) and mixed greens. Sodium: 200mg, Potassium: 365mg, Phosphorus: 180mg.
- **Snack:** A small serving of watermelon. Sodium: 2mg, Potassium: 170mg, Phosphorus: 11mg.
- **Dinner:** Baked cod with roasted Brussels sprouts and a small serving of brown rice. Sodium: 300mg, Potassium: 600mg, Phosphorus: 220mg.
- **Dessert:** A small bunch of red grapes. Sodium: 2mg, Potassium: 176mg, Phosphorus: 15mg.

Day 9:

- **Breakfast:** A serving of unsweetened muesli with almond milk. Sodium: 50mg, Potassium: 200mg, Phosphorus: 125mg.
- **Snack:** A small orange. Sodium: 0mg, Potassium: 181mg, Phosphorus: 18mg.
- **Lunch:** Baked chicken breast with steamed broccoli and a quinoa salad. Sodium: 220mg, Potassium: 400mg, Phosphorus: 220mg.
- **Snack:** A small banana. Sodium: 1mg, Potassium: 422mg, Phosphorus: 26mg.
- **Dinner:** Grilled tilapia with mashed sweet potato and green beans. Sodium: 250mg, Potassium: 650mg, Phosphorus: 200mg.
- **Dessert:** A small serving of fresh pineapple. Sodium: 1mg, Potassium: 120mg, Phosphorus: 10mg.

Day 10:

- **Breakfast:** A bowl of oatmeal (made with water) topped with a sprinkle of cinnamon. Sodium: 115mg, Potassium: 170mg, Phosphorus: 180mg.
- **Snack:** A serving of canned peaches (in water). Sodium: 10mg, Potassium: 160mg, Phosphorus: 15mg.
- **Lunch:** Tuna salad (with light mayo) on whole grain bread, served with sliced cucumbers. Sodium: 300mg, Potassium: 300mg, Phosphorus: 200mg.
- **Snack:** A small handful of seedless grapes. Sodium: 1mg, Potassium: 100mg, Phosphorus: 10mg.
- **Dinner:** Roasted turkey breast with a side of steamed zucchini and quinoa. Sodium: 400mg, Potassium: 450mg, Phosphorus: 220mg.
- **Dessert:** A small serving of apple slices. Sodium: 1mg, Potassium: 85mg, Phosphorus: 8mg.

Day 11:

- **Breakfast:** Scrambled egg whites with a side of fresh berries. Sodium: 120mg, Potassium: 150mg, Phosphorus: 120mg.
- **Snack:** A small banana. Sodium: 1mg, Potassium: 422mg, Phosphorus: 26mg.
- **Lunch:** Grilled chicken salad with mixed greens, cherry tomatoes, and light dressing. Sodium: 220mg, Potassium: 400mg, Phosphorus: 180mg.
- **Snack:** A small serving of fresh pineapple. Sodium: 1mg, Potassium: 120mg, Phosphorus: 10mg.
- **Dinner:** Baked salmon with a squeeze of lemon, served with steamed carrots and brown rice. Sodium: 300mg, Potassium: 500mg, Phosphorus: 240mg.
- **Dessert:** A small serving of cantaloupe. Sodium: 2mg, Potassium: 267mg, Phosphorus: 12mg.

Day 12:

- **Breakfast:** A bowl of grits with a side of fresh blueberries. Sodium: 110mg, Potassium: 114mg, Phosphorus: 91mg.
- **Snack:** A small pear. Sodium: 1mg, Potassium: 206mg, Phosphorus: 20mg.
- **Lunch:** Tofu stir-fry with a variety of colorful veggies and a side of brown rice. Sodium: 330mg, Potassium: 300mg, Phosphorus: 240mg.
- **Snack:** A small serving of fresh strawberries. Sodium: 1mg, Potassium: 220mg, Phosphorus: 20mg.
- **Dinner:** Grilled shrimp skewers with steamed green beans and couscous. Sodium: 370mg, Potassium: 400mg, Phosphorus: 240mg.
- **Dessert:** A handful of fresh blackberries. Sodium: 1mg, Potassium: 233mg, Phosphorus: 32mg.

Day 13:

- **Breakfast:** Pancakes (made with egg whites) with a drizzle of sugar-free syrup. Sodium: 410mg, Potassium: 200mg, Phosphorus: 120mg.
- **Snack:** A small kiwi. Sodium: 2mg, Potassium: 215mg, Phosphorus: 25mg.
- **Lunch:** Veggie wrap with hummus, served with cucumber slices. Sodium: 250mg, Potassium: 300mg, Phosphorus: 120mg.
- **Snack:** A serving of unsalted almond slices. Sodium: 0mg, Potassium: 200mg, Phosphorus: 160mg.
- **Dinner:** Baked chicken with roasted sweet potatoes and steamed Brussels sprouts. Sodium: 400mg, Potassium: 800mg, Phosphorus: 300mg.
- **Dessert:** A small slice of watermelon. Sodium: 2mg, Potassium: 170mg, Phosphorus: 11mg.

Day 14:

- **Breakfast:** Whole grain cereal with almond milk. Sodium: 150mg, Potassium: 160mg, Phosphorus: 100mg.
- **Snack:** A small serving of fresh blueberries. Sodium: 1mg, Potassium: 114mg, Phosphorus: 18mg.
- **Lunch:** Turkey and cheese sandwich on whole wheat bread with baby carrots. Sodium: 400mg, Potassium: 350mg, Phosphorus: 200mg.
- **Snack:** A small handful of seedless grapes. Sodium: 1mg, Potassium: 100mg, Phosphorus: 10mg.
- **Dinner:** Grilled trout with boiled green beans and white rice. Sodium: 350mg, Potassium: 500mg, Phosphorus: 240mg.
- **Dessert:** A small serving of diced cantaloupe. Sodium: 2mg, Potassium: 267mg, Phosphorus: 12mg.

Day 15:

- **Breakfast:** Omelette made with egg whites and spinach. Sodium: 200mg, Potassium: 220mg, Phosphorus: 100mg.
- **Snack:** A small apple. Sodium: 1mg, Potassium: 148mg, Phosphorus: 10mg.
- **Lunch:** Grilled chicken Caesar salad (light on dressing) with cherry tomatoes. Sodium: 320mg, Potassium: 400mg, Phosphorus: 180mg.
- **Snack:** A small serving of fresh raspberries. Sodium: 1mg, Potassium: 186mg, Phosphorus: 30mg.
- **Dinner:** Baked pork chop with a side of steamed asparagus and couscous. Sodium: 420mg, Potassium: 600mg, Phosphorus: 280mg.
- **Dessert:** A small serving of fresh pineapple. Sodium: 1mg, Potassium: 120mg, Phosphorus: 10mg.

Day 16:

- **Breakfast:** Whole-grain toast with almond butter. Sodium: 160mg, Potassium: 210mg, Phosphorus: 120mg.
- **Snack:** A small serving of fresh strawberries. Sodium: 1mg, Potassium: 170mg, Phosphorus: 15mg.
- **Lunch:** Baked salmon salad with light dressing and a side of cucumber slices. Sodium: 280mg, Potassium: 400mg, Phosphorus: 240mg.
- **Snack:** A small orange. Sodium: 0mg, Potassium: 181mg, Phosphorus: 18mg.
- **Dinner:** Roasted turkey with a side of steamed cauliflower and quinoa. Sodium: 350mg, Potassium: 450mg, Phosphorus: 220mg.
- **Dessert:** A small serving of fresh blackberries. Sodium: 1mg, Potassium: 144mg, Phosphorus: 20mg.

Day 17:

- **Breakfast:** Unsweetened muesli with almond milk. Sodium: 70mg, Potassium: 200mg, Phosphorus: 150mg.
- **Snack:** A small pear. Sodium: 1mg, Potassium: 206mg, Phosphorus: 20mg.
- **Lunch:** Veggie wrap with hummus, served with sliced bell peppers. Sodium: 220mg, Potassium: 300mg, Phosphorus: 130mg.
- **Snack:** A small serving of fresh pineapple. Sodium: 1mg, Potassium: 120mg, Phosphorus: 10mg.
- **Dinner:** Baked chicken with a side of roasted zucchini and sweet potatoes. Sodium: 400mg, Potassium: 700mg, Phosphorus: 280mg.
- **Dessert:** A small serving of fresh blueberries. Sodium: 1mg, Potassium: 114mg, Phosphorus: 18mg.

Day 18:

- **Breakfast:** A bowl of oatmeal (made with water) sprinkled with fresh raspberries. Sodium: 115mg, Potassium: 190mg, Phosphorus: 180mg.
- **Snack:** A small banana. Sodium: 1mg, Potassium: 422mg, Phosphorus: 26mg.
- **Lunch:** Tuna salad (with light mayo) on whole grain bread, served with sliced cucumbers. Sodium: 300mg, Potassium: 300mg, Phosphorus: 200mg.
- **Snack:** A small serving of fresh strawberry slices. Sodium: 1mg, Potassium: 220mg, Phosphorus: 15mg.
- **Dinner:** Grilled shrimp with a side of steamed broccoli and couscous. Sodium: 370mg, Potassium: 400mg, Phosphorus: 220mg.
- **Dessert:** A small serving of diced cantaloupe. Sodium: 2mg, Potassium: 267mg, Phosphorus: 12mg.

Day 19:

- **Breakfast:** Whole wheat toast with avocado. Sodium: 150mg, Potassium: 240mg, Phosphorus: 100mg.
- **Snack:** A small serving of fresh strawberries. Sodium: 1mg, Potassium: 114mg, Phosphorus: 18mg.
- **Lunch:** Roasted turkey sandwich with lettuce and tomato on whole grain bread. Sodium: 300mg, Potassium: 300mg, Phosphorus: 200mg.
- **Snack:** A small orange. Sodium: 0mg, Potassium: 181mg, Phosphorus: 18mg.
- **Dinner:** Baked tilapia with a side of steamed green beans and couscous. Sodium: 200mg, Potassium: 400mg, Phosphorus: 200mg.
- **Dessert:** A small serving of fresh raspberries. Sodium: 1mg, Potassium: 186mg, Phosphorus: 30mg.

Day 20:

- **Breakfast:** Scrambled eggs (using egg whites) with spinach. Sodium: 200mg, Potassium: 200mg, Phosphorus: 120mg.
- **Snack:** A small banana. Sodium: 1mg, Potassium: 422mg, Phosphorus: 26mg.
- **Lunch:** Tofu stir-fry with various colorful vegetables, served over brown rice. Sodium: 330mg, Potassium: 300mg, Phosphorus: 240mg.
- **Snack:** A small serving of fresh melon slices. Sodium: 2mg, Potassium: 170mg, Phosphorus: 15mg.
- **Dinner:** Roasted chicken with a side of steamed broccoli and quinoa. Sodium: 400mg, Potassium: 500mg, Phosphorus: 240mg.
- **Dessert:** A small apple. Sodium: 1mg, Potassium: 148mg, Phosphorus: 10mg.

Day 21:

- **Breakfast:** Quinoa porridge with a sprinkle of cinnamon. Sodium: 160mg, Potassium: 180mg, Phosphorus: 120mg.
- **Snack:** A small serving of fresh blackberries. Sodium: 1mg, Potassium: 144mg, Phosphorus: 20mg.
- **Lunch:** Baked cod with a side of sautéed spinach and brown rice. Sodium: 320mg, Potassium: 350mg, Phosphorus: 210mg.
- **Snack:** A small pear. Sodium: 1mg, Potassium: 206mg, Phosphorus: 20mg.
- **Dinner:** Roasted turkey breast with steamed green beans and couscous. Sodium: 350mg, Potassium: 450mg, Phosphorus: 220mg.
- **Dessert:** A small serving of fresh kiwi fruit. Sodium: 2mg, Potassium: 237mg, Phosphorus: 25mg.

Day 22:

- **Breakfast:** Oatmeal (made with water) with a handful of blueberries. Sodium: 120mg, Potassium: 190mg, Phosphorus: 180mg.
- **Snack:** A small serving of fresh strawberries. Sodium: 1mg, Potassium: 170mg, Phosphorus: 15mg.
- **Lunch:** Grilled chicken salad with light dressing, served with sliced cucumbers. Sodium: 280mg, Potassium: 400mg, Phosphorus: 240mg.
- **Snack:** A small orange. Sodium: 0mg, Potassium: 181mg, Phosphorus: 18mg.
- **Dinner:** Baked tilapia with a side of steamed asparagus and quinoa. Sodium: 250mg, Potassium: 450mg, Phosphorus: 240mg.
- **Dessert:** A small serving of fresh pineapple chunks. Sodium: 1mg, Potassium: 120mg, Phosphorus: 10mg.

Day 23:

- **Breakfast:** Whole wheat toast with a thin layer of peanut butter. Sodium: 200mg, Potassium: 190mg, Phosphorus: 100mg.
- **Snack:** A small serving of fresh grapes. Sodium: 1mg, Potassium: 176mg, Phosphorus: 15mg.
- **Lunch:** Grilled turkey salad with light dressing and a side of sliced cucumbers. Sodium: 350mg, Potassium: 350mg, Phosphorus: 220mg.
- **Snack:** A small apple. Sodium: 1mg, Potassium: 148mg, Phosphorus: 10mg.
- **Dinner:** Baked salmon with a side of steamed cauliflower and couscous. Sodium: 300mg, Potassium: 400mg, Phosphorus: 200mg.
- **Dessert:** A small serving of fresh blueberries. Sodium: 1mg, Potassium: 114mg, Phosphorus: 18mg.

Day 24:

- **Breakfast:** Veggie omelet with mushrooms and spinach. Sodium: 150mg, Potassium: 250mg, Phosphorus: 120mg.
- **Snack:** A small serving of diced cantaloupe. Sodium: 2mg, Potassium: 267mg, Phosphorus: 12mg.
- **Lunch:** Tofu stir-fry with bell peppers and broccoli, served over brown rice. Sodium: 330mg, Potassium: 400mg, Phosphorus: 200mg.
- **Snack:** A small banana. Sodium: 1mg, Potassium: 422mg, Phosphorus: 26mg.
- **Dinner:** Grilled shrimp with a side of steamed green beans and quinoa. Sodium: 400mg, Potassium: 450mg, Phosphorus: 220mg.
- **Dessert:** A small serving of fresh raspberries. Sodium: 1mg, Potassium: 186mg, Phosphorus: 30mg.

Day 25:

- **Breakfast:** A bowl of cream of wheat with a small drizzle of honey. Sodium: 120mg, Potassium: 170mg, Phosphorus: 50mg.
- **Snack:** A small serving of fresh mango slices. Sodium: 1mg, Potassium: 168mg, Phosphorus: 14mg.
- **Lunch:** Grilled fish with a side of steamed zucchini and couscous. Sodium: 340mg, Potassium: 370mg, Phosphorus: 190mg.
- **Snack:** A small peach. Sodium: 0mg, Potassium: 285mg, Phosphorus: 15mg.
- **Dinner:** Roasted turkey with a side of steamed carrots and brown rice. Sodium: 360mg, Potassium: 450mg, Phosphorus: 250mg.
- **Dessert:** A small serving of fresh strawberries. Sodium: 1mg, Potassium: 220mg, Phosphorus: 32mg.

Day 26:

- **Breakfast:** Scrambled eggs (using egg whites) with a slice of whole grain toast. Sodium: 220mg, Potassium: 210mg, Phosphorus: 140mg.
- **Snack:** A small serving of fresh blackberries. Sodium: 1mg, Potassium: 144mg, Phosphorus: 20mg.
- **Lunch:** Tofu salad with a light vinaigrette, served with sliced cucumbers. Sodium: 260mg, Potassium: 320mg, Phosphorus: 220mg.
- **Snack:** A small apple. Sodium: 1mg, Potassium: 148mg, Phosphorus: 10mg.
- **Dinner:** Baked chicken with a side of steamed green beans and quinoa. Sodium: 400mg, Potassium: 370mg, Phosphorus: 240mg.
- **Dessert:** A small serving of fresh blueberries. Sodium: 1mg, Potassium: 114mg, Phosphorus: 18mg.

Day 27:

- **Breakfast:** A bowl of grits with a small pat of butter. Sodium: 240mg, Potassium: 91mg, Phosphorus: 5mg.
- **Snack:** A small serving of fresh pineapple chunks. Sodium: 1mg, Potassium: 120mg, Phosphorus: 10mg.
- **Lunch:** Baked cod with a side of sautéed spinach and couscous. Sodium: 320mg, Potassium: 350mg, Phosphorus: 210mg.
- **Snack:** A small pear. Sodium: 1mg, Potassium: 206mg, Phosphorus: 20mg.
- **Dinner:** Roasted pork loin with steamed broccoli and brown rice. Sodium: 350mg, Potassium: 510mg, Phosphorus: 220mg.
- **Dessert:** A small serving of fresh raspberry. Sodium: 1mg, Potassium: 186mg, Phosphorus: 30mg.

Day 28:

- **Breakfast:** A bowl of oatmeal topped with a small handful of dried cranberries. Sodium: 115mg, Potassium: 180mg, Phosphorus: 105mg.
- **Snack:** A small serving of fresh orange slices. Sodium: 0mg, Potassium: 237mg, Phosphorus: 18mg.
- **Lunch:** Grilled turkey cutlets with steamed Brussels sprouts and barley. Sodium: 220mg, Potassium: 400mg, Phosphorus: 240mg.
- **Snack:** A small plum. Sodium: 0mg, Potassium: 104mg, Phosphorus: 16mg.
- **Dinner:** Baked trout with a side of steamed asparagus and millet. Sodium: 260mg, Potassium: 440mg, Phosphorus: 235mg.
- **Dessert:** A small serving of fresh cherries. Sodium: 0mg, Potassium: 260mg, Phosphorus: 15mg.

Day 29:

- **Breakfast:** Whole grain toast with a thin layer of almond butter. Sodium: 150mg, Potassium: 200mg, Phosphorus: 120mg.
- **Snack:** A small serving of fresh grapes. Sodium: 1mg, Potassium: 176mg, Phosphorus: 15mg.
- **Lunch:** Baked chicken breast with steamed summer squash and couscous. Sodium: 280mg, Potassium: 350mg, Phosphorus: 170mg.
- **Snack:** A small apple. Sodium: 1mg, Potassium: 148mg, Phosphorus: 10mg.
- **Dinner:** Steamed tilapia with a side of roasted cauliflower and quinoa. Sodium: 200mg, Potassium: 500mg, Phosphorus: 240mg.
- **Dessert:** A small serving of fresh strawberries. Sodium: 1mg, Potassium: 170mg, Phosphorus: 15mg.

Day 30:

- **Breakfast:** A bowl of Cream of Rice with a drizzle of honey. Sodium: 95mg, Potassium: 177mg, Phosphorus: 55mg.
- **Snack:** A small serving of fresh blackberries. Sodium: 1mg, Potassium: 144mg, Phosphorus: 20mg.
- **Lunch:** Grilled salmon with roasted Brussels sprouts and brown rice. Sodium: 300mg, Potassium: 400mg, Phosphorus: 250mg.
- **Snack:** A small peach. Sodium: 0mg, Potassium: 285mg, Phosphorus: 15mg.
- **Dinner:** Roasted turkey with a side of steamed green beans and barley. Sodium: 250mg, Potassium: 450mg, Phosphorus: 240mg.
- **Dessert:** A small serving of fresh raspberries. Sodium: 1mg, Potassium: 186mg, Phosphorus: 30mg.

It's important to reflect on the changes we've made and how they have positively impacted our overall health. By incorporating more low-sodium, low-potassium, and low-phosphorus foods into our diet, we have not only supported our kidney function but also improved our overall well-being.

Remember, following a kidney-friendly diet doesn't mean sacrificing flavor or variety in our meals. With the help of fresh fruits and vegetables, lean proteins, and whole grains, we can still enjoy a wide range of delicious and nutritious foods.

In addition to diet, it's also important to stay hydrated by drinking plenty of water throughout the day. This helps our kidneys function properly and flush out toxins from our body.

Overall, making small changes to our daily eating habits can have a big impact on our kidney health. Let's continue to make smart choices and prioritize our well-being for a healthier future.

4

KEY FOODS TO INCLUDE IN YOUR DIET

In addition to following a well-balanced meal plan, certain foods and nutrients are especially beneficial for seniors with kidney disease. This chapter will discuss what foods are suitable for your kidney-friendly diet.

Overview of Beneficial Foods

Whole Grains: Whole grains, such as brown rice, oatmeal, and whole wheat bread, are an excellent source of dietary fiber, essential in maintaining digestive health. They are also packed with B vitamins, iron, and other minerals contributing to overall wellness. Whole grains are more satisfying than refined grains, helping to control appetite and maintain a healthy weight.

Fresh Fruits and Vegetables: Fresh fruits and vegetables are nutritional powerhouses, rich in vitamins, minerals, antioxidants, and dietary fiber. They offer a broad spectrum of health benefits, from boosting the immune system to reducing the risk of chronic diseases. Different types of fruits and vegetables provide varying nutrients, so including a colorful variety in your diet is beneficial.

Lean Proteins: Lean proteins, such as chicken, turkey, fish, eggs, and low-fat dairy products, are essential for muscle growth and repair. They also play a crucial role in immune function and creating hormones. Consuming lean proteins instead of fatty meats can help control weight and reduce the risk of heart disease and other health conditions.

Healthy Carbs: Contrary to popular belief, not all carbs are bad. Healthy carbs, or complex carbohydrates, include whole grains, legumes, fruits, and vegetables. These carbs are absorbed slowly into our systems, avoiding spikes in blood sugar levels, and are packed with fiber, keeping you satiated longer. They are the body's primary energy source, fueling the brain, kidneys, and muscles during physical activity.

Although these food groups are beneficial, it's important to remember that a balanced diet is key. This means consuming enough nutrients from various food sources to maintain optimal health. Consulting with a healthcare provider or dietitian is highly recommended when making changes to your diet.

List of Food Items to Enjoy While on a Kidney-Friendly Diet

- **Omega-3 Fatty Acids:** Foods rich in Omega-3 fatty acids, such as salmon, mackerel, and chia seeds, can help reduce inflammation and improve kidney function.
- **Salmon:** A 3-ounce serving of cooked salmon has approximately: **Sodium:** 50mg, **Potassium:** 363mg, and **Phosphorus:** 274mg.
- **Mackerel:** In a 3-ounce serving of cooked Atlantic mackerel, there is approximately **Sodium:** 90mg, **Potassium:** 314mg, and **Phosphorus:** 252mg.
- **Chia Seeds:** One ounce of Chia seeds contains: **Sodium:** 5mg, **Potassium:** 115mg, and **Phosphorus:** 265mg.

- **Red Bell Peppers:** Low potassium and high in flavor, perfect for the kidney diet. They're also an excellent source of vitamins C and A, as well as vitamin B6, folic acid, and fiber. One medium red bell pepper (119g) contains approximately: **Sodium:** 3mg, **Potassium:** 251mg, and **Phosphorus:** 31mg.
- **Cabbage:** Cabbage is a kidney-friendly veggie naturally low in sodium, potassium, and phosphorus. This cruciferous vegetable is also packed with vitamins K, C, and many B vitamins. One cup of chopped raw cabbage (89g) contains approximately: **Sodium:** 13mg, **potassium:** 119mg, and **Phosphorus:** 18mg.
- **Cauliflower:** Cauliflower is a versatile and nutrient-rich vegetable well-tolerated by many individuals with stage 3 Chronic Kidney Disease (CKD). It is a crucial source of Vitamin C, Vitamin K, and folate. Additionally, it's low in potassium, sodium, and phosphorus, making it kidney-friendly. One cup of chopped raw cauliflower (107g) contains approximately: **Sodium:** 30mg, **Potassium:** 320mg, and **Phosphorus:** 45mg.
- **Blueberries:** Blueberries have antioxidant properties and are low in sodium, potassium, and phosphorus - vital for individuals with stage 3 CKD. They also provide a substantial amount of Vitamin C and fiber. One cup of fresh blueberries (148g) contains approximately: **Sodium:** 1mg, **Potassium:** 114mg, and **Phosphorus:** 18mg.
- **Egg Whites:** Egg whites are pure protein and provide the highest quality protein with all the essential amino acids. For the kidney diet, egg whites provide protein with less phosphorus than other protein sources such as egg yolk or meats. Two large egg whites (66g) contain approximately: **Sodium:** 110mg, **Potassium:** 108mg, and **Phosphorus:** 10mg.
- **Apples:** Apples are high in fiber, have anti-inflammatory properties, and can help reduce cholesterol. They're also relatively low in potassium, sodium, and phosphorus, making them an excellent choice for seniors with stage 3

CKD. One medium apple (182g) contains approximately: **Sodium:** 2mg, **Potassium:** 195mg, and **Phosphorus:** 20mg.

- **Pineapple:** Known for its sweet, tangy flavor, pineapples make a great option for those on a kidney-friendly diet. They contain less potassium than other fruits and offer a healthy dose of vitamins and fiber. One cup of pineapple chunks (165g) contains approximately: **Sodium:** 2mg, **Potassium:** 180mg, and **Phosphorus:** 13mg.
- **Cranberries:** Cranberries are great for preventing urinary tract infections and are very low in potassium, making them suitable for those with stage 3 CKD. One cup of fresh cranberries (100g) contains approximately: **Sodium:** 2mg, **Potassium:** 85mg, and **Phosphorus:** 13mg.
- **Turnips:** Turnips are a great replacement for vegetables that are higher in potassium, like potatoes and winter squash. They are also a good source of Vitamin C. One cup of cubed raw turnips (130g) contains approximately: **Sodium:** 87mg, **Potassium:** 233mg, and **Phosphorus:** 42mg.
- **Strawberries:** Strawberries are a delicious, kidney-friendly fruit with a significant amount of fiber and Vitamin C. They are also low in sodium, potassium, and phosphorus. One cup of fresh strawberries (152g) contains approximately: **Sodium:** 2mg, **Potassium:** 254mg, and **Phosphorus:** 35mg.
- **Rice:** Rice, particularly white rice, is a good source of energy and B vitamins and is low in sodium, potassium, and phosphorus, making it suitable for individuals with stage 3 CKD. One cup of cooked white rice (158g) contains approximately: **Sodium:** 4mg, **Potassium:** 52mg, and **Phosphorus:** 69mg.
- **Cucumber:** Known for its hydration properties, cucumbers are also low in potassium, sodium, and phosphorus. They are a good choice for those on a kidney-friendly diet. One medium cucumber (201g) contains approximately: **Sodium:** 2mg, **Potassium:** 442mg, and **Phosphorus:** 54mg.

- **Onions:** Onions are flavorful and packed with beneficial antioxidants and Vitamin C. They are also low in potassium, making them a kidney-friendly ingredient. One medium onion (110g) contains approximately: **Sodium:** 4mg, **Potassium:** 190mg, and **Phosphorus:** 35mg.
- **Garlic:** Garlic adds flavor to dishes and has many health benefits, including reducing blood pressure and cholesterol. It's also low in sodium, potassium, and phosphorus. Three cloves of garlic (9g) contain approximately: **Sodium:** 2mg, **Potassium:** 36mg, and **Phosphorus:** 14mg.
- **Radishes:** Radishes are crisp, delicious, and low in sodium, potassium, and phosphorus. They make a great addition to salads and dishes, adding flavor without the added risk for those on a kidney-friendly diet. One cup of sliced radishes (116g) contains approximately: **Sodium:** 45mg, **Potassium:** 270mg, and **Phosphorus:** 23mg.
- **Blackberries:** Blackberries are rich in antioxidants and vitamins. They're also low in sodium, potassium, and phosphorus, making them a great snack choice for those with stage 3 CKD. One cup of fresh blackberries (144g) contains approximately: **Sodium:** 1mg, **Potassium:** 233mg, and **Phosphorus:** 32mg.
- **Green Beans:** Green beans are an excellent source of vitamins A, C, and K and are low in potassium, sodium, and phosphorus. One cup of raw green beans (100g) contains approximately: **Sodium:** 6mg, **Potassium:** 211mg, and **Phosphorus:** 38mg.
- **Carrots:** Carrots are not only tasty and versatile but also offer a good dose of vitamins and fiber. They're low in sodium, potassium, and phosphorus, making them suitable for a kidney-friendly diet. One medium carrot (61g) contains approximately: **Sodium:** 42mg, **Potassium:** 195mg, and **Phosphorus:** 25mg.
- **Raspberries:** Raspberries are a delicious fruit high in dietary fiber and vitamin C. They are low in sodium, potassium, and

phosphorus, making them an ideal snack for individuals with CKD. One cup of fresh raspberries (123g) contains approximately: **Sodium:** 1mg, **Potassium:** 186mg, and **Phosphorus:** 29mg.

- **Cabbage:** Cabbage is a versatile vegetable, high in vitamins K and C and fiber. It's low in potassium, sodium, and phosphorus, making it a good choice for those with stage 3 CKD. One cup of chopped raw cabbage (89g) contains approximately: **Sodium:** 13mg, **Potassium:** 119mg and **Phosphorus:** 18mg.

- **Bell Peppers:** Bell peppers are rich in flavor and packed with vitamins A, C, and B6. They are low in potassium and phosphorus, which benefits those on a kidney-friendly diet. One medium bell pepper (119g) contains approximately: **Sodium:** 3mg, **Potassium:** 251mg, and **Phosphorus:** 26mg.

- **Grapes:** Grapes are refreshing and full of antioxidants, especially the red and purple varieties. They're low in phosphorus and potassium, which makes them a safe snack for individuals with stage 3 CKD. One cup of grapes (151g) contains approximately: **Sodium:** 3mg, **Potassium:** 288mg, and **Phosphorus:** 30mg.

- **Cauliflower:** Cauliflower is high in vitamin C and a good source of folate and fiber. It's also low in potassium, sodium, and phosphorus. One cup of chopped raw cauliflower (107g) contains approximately: **Sodium:** 30mg, **Potassium:** 320mg, and **Phosphorus:** 45mg.

- **Olive Oil:** Olive oil is a healthy source of fat and is excellent for heart health. It's also low in sodium, potassium, and phosphorus, making it safe for individuals with stage 3 CKD. One tablespoon of olive oil (14g) contains approximately: **Sodium:** 0.6mg, **Potassium:** 0.3mg, and **Phosphorus:** 0mg.

- **Popcorn:** Popcorn is a low-phosphorus snack for those on a kidney-friendly diet. Three cups of air-popped popcorn (24g) contain approximately: **Sodium:** 2mg, **Potassium:** 26mg, and **Phosphorus:** 22mg.

- **Strawberries**: Strawberries are full of antioxidants and vitamin C. They have low sodium, potassium, and phosphorus levels, making them a great choice for those with stage 3 CKD. One cup of fresh strawberries (152g) contains approximately: **Sodium**: 1.5mg, **Potassium**: 220mg, and **Phosphorus**: 35mg.
- **Zucchini**: Zucchini is a versatile vegetable high in vitamin C and fiber. It's low in sodium, potassium, and phosphorus, making it ideal for a kidney-friendly diet. One medium zucchini (196g) contains approximately: **Sodium**: 16mg, **Potassium**: 512mg, and **Phosphorus**: 78mg.
- **Cranberries**: Cranberries are tart and packed with antioxidants. They're low in sodium, potassium, and phosphorus, making them suitable for those with stage 3 CKD. One cup of fresh cranberries (100g) contains approximately: **Sodium**: 2mg, **Potassium**: 85mg, and **Phosphorus**: 13mg.
- **Cucumber**: Cucumbers are refreshing and low in sodium, potassium, and phosphorus. One medium cucumber (201g) contains approximately: **Sodium**: 6mg, **Potassium**: 442mg, and **Phosphorus**: 72mg.
- **Almonds**: Almonds are a good source of healthy fats and protein. They have low sodium but moderate levels of potassium and phosphorus. A serving of 1 ounce (28g) contains approximately: **Sodium**: 1mg, **Potassium**: 200mg, and **Phosphorus**: 137mg.
- **Tofu**: Tofu is a great source of plant-based protein and is low in sodium, potassium, and phosphorus. A 3.5-ounce (100g) serving of tofu contains approximately: Sodium: 9mg, **Potassium**: 144mg, and **Phosphorus**: 97mg.
- **Rice Milk**: Rice milk is a low sodium, potassium, and phosphorus alternative to dairy milk. One cup (240g) of rice milk contains approximately: **Sodium**: 100mg, **Potassium**: 80mg, and **Phosphorus**: 23mg.

- **White Bread:** White bread is a lower phosphorus alternative to whole grain bread. One slice (28g) contains approximately: **Sodium:** 170mg, **Potassium:** 35mg, and **Phosphorus:** 25mg.
- **Honeydew Melon:** Honeydew melon is sweet and refreshing, and it's low in sodium, potassium, and phosphorus. One cup of diced honeydew (170g) contains approximately: **Sodium:** 18mg, **Potassium:** 404mg, and **Phosphorus:** 14mg.
- **Macadamia Nuts:** Macadamia nuts are high in healthy fats and a good source of protein. They're also low in sodium, potassium, and phosphorus. A 1-ounce serving (28g) contains approximately: **Sodium:** 1mg, **Potassium:** 104mg, and **Phosphorus:** 53mg.
- **Carrots:** Carrots are rich in beta-carotene and vitamin A. They're low in sodium, potassium, and phosphorus, making them a good choice for those with stage 3 CKD. One medium carrot (61g) contains approximately: **Sodium:** 42mg, **Potassium:** 195mg, and **Phosphorus:** 25mg.
- **Watermelon:** Watermelons are hydrating and contain vitamins A and C. They have low sodium, potassium, and phosphorus content, making them an ideal choice for those with stage 3 CKD. One cup of diced watermelon (152g) contains approximately: **Sodium:** 2mg, **Potassium:** 170mg, and **Phosphorus:** 11mg.
- **Raspberries:** Raspberries are rich in fiber and vitamins C and K. They are low in sodium, potassium, and phosphorus. One cup of fresh raspberries (123g) contains approximately: **Sodium:** 1mg, **Potassium:** 186mg, and **Phosphorus:** 29mg.
- **Cherry Tomatoes (in moderation):** Cherry tomatoes are sweet, tangy, and low in sodium, potassium, and phosphorus. They are also a good source of vitamins A, C, and K. One cup of cherry tomatoes (149g) contains approximately: **Sodium:** 9mg, **Potassium:** 353mg, and **Phosphorus:** 36mg.
- **White Rice:** White rice is a staple food that is lower in potassium and phosphorus than brown rice. One cup of

cooked white rice (186g) contains approximately: **Sodium:** 4mg, **Potassium:** 55mg, and **Phosphorus:** 68mg.

- **Shiitake Mushrooms:** Shiitake mushrooms are a flavorful addition to meals and are low in sodium, potassium, and phosphorus. A half cup of cooked shiitake mushrooms (72g) contains approximately: **Sodium:** 3mg, **Potassium:** 214mg, and **Phosphorus:** 42mg.
- **Pears:** Pears are a good source of fiber and vitamin C, and they're low in potassium and phosphorus. One medium pear (178g) contains approximately: **Sodium:** 2mg, **Potassium:** 206mg, and **Phosphorus:** 24mg.
- **Endive:** Endive is a leafy green vegetable low in sodium, potassium, and phosphorus. One cup of chopped endive (50g) contains approximately: **Sodium:** 11mg, **Potassium:** 157mg, and **Phosphorus:** 14mg.
- **Scallops:** Scallops are a lean source of protein and are low in sodium, potassium, and phosphorus. Three ounces of cooked scallops (84g) contain approximately: **Sodium** 567mg, **Potassium** 285mg, and **Phosphorus** 186mg.
- **Kale:** Kale is a nutrient-dense leafy green low in sodium, potassium, and phosphorus. One cup of chopped raw kale (67g) contains approximately: **Sodium:** 29mg, **Potassium:** 299mg, and **Phosphorus:** 37mg.
- **Chicken Breast (small portions):** Chicken breast is a lean source of protein and is low in sodium, potassium, and phosphorus. Three ounces of roasted chicken breast (85g) contains approximately: **Sodium:** 64mg, **Potassium:** 220mg, and **Phosphorus:** 196mg.
- **Arugula (portion control):** Arugula is a nutrient-dense leafy green low in sodium, potassium, and phosphorus. One cup of raw arugula (20g) contains approximately: **Sodium:** 13mg, **Potassium:** 74mg, and **Phosphorus:** 8mg.
- **Cod:** Cod is a lean source of protein and is low in sodium, potassium, and phosphorus. Three ounces of cooked cod

(85g) contains approximately: **Sodium:** 74mg, **Potassium:** 439mg, and **Phosphorus:** 176mg.

- **Shrimp (unfrozen):** Shrimp is a lean protein source low in sodium, potassium, and phosphorus. Three ounces of cooked shrimp (85g) contains approximately: **Sodium:** 123mg, **Potassium:** 185mg, and **Phosphorus:** 163mg.

- **Asparagus:** Asparagus is a spring vegetable that's a good source of vitamin K. It's low in sodium, potassium, and phosphorus. One cup of raw asparagus (134g) contains approximately: **Sodium:** 2mg, **Potassium:** 202mg, and **Phosphorus:** 70mg.

- **Eggplant:** Eggplant is a versatile vegetable low in sodium, potassium, and phosphorus. One cup of raw eggplant (82g) contains approximately: **Sodium:** 2mg, **Potassium:** 188mg, and **Phosphorus:** 15mg.

- **Collard Greens (portion control):** Collard greens are a nutrient-rich leafy green low in sodium, potassium, and phosphorus. One cup of raw collard greens (36g) contains approximately: **Sodium:** 6mg, **Potassium:** 77mg, and **Phosphorus:** 15mg.

- **Turkey Breast (portion control):** Turkey breast is a lean source of protein and low in sodium, potassium, and phosphorus. Three ounces of roasted turkey breast (85g) contains approximately: **Sodium:** 50mg, **Potassium:** 224mg, and **Phosphorus:** 192mg.

- **Plums:** Plums are a good source of vitamin C and are low in sodium, potassium, and phosphorus. One medium plum (66g) contains approximately: **Sodium:** 0mg, **Potassium:** 104mg, and **Phosphorus:** 12mg.

- **Mushrooms:** Mushrooms are low in sodium, potassium, and phosphorus, making them a good choice for those on a stage 3 CKD diet. One cup of raw, whole mushrooms (96g) contains approximately: **Sodium:** 5mg, **Potassium:** 223mg, and **Phosphorus:** 82mg.

- **Snow Peas**: Snow peas are a crisp, sweet vegetable low in sodium, potassium, and phosphorus. One cup of raw snow peas (98g) contains approximately: **Sodium:** 4mg, **Potassium:** 160mg, and **Phosphorus:** 54mg.
- **Celery**: Celery is a crunchy vegetable low in sodium, potassium, and phosphorus. One medium stalk of celery (40g) contains approximately: **Sodium:** 32mg, **Potassium:** 104mg, and **Phosphorus:** 11mg.
- **Pumpkin (small amounts)**: Pumpkin is a vitamin A-rich vegetable low in sodium, potassium, and phosphorus. One cup of cooked, mashed pumpkin (245g) contains approximately: **Sodium:** 2mg, **Potassium:** 564mg, and **Phosphorus:** 73mg.
- **Apricots**: Apricots are a fruit high in vitamins A and C and low in sodium, potassium, and phosphorus. One medium fresh apricot (35g) contains approximately: **Sodium:** 1mg, **Potassium:** 91mg, and **Phosphorus:** 8mg.
- **Milk (Non-Dairy, Almond)**: Almond milk, unsweetened, is a fantastic alternative to dairy for those on a kidney-friendly diet. One cup of almond milk (240g) contains approximately: **Sodium:** 186mg, **Potassium:** 160mg, and **Phosphorus:** 24mg.
- **Cheese (Swiss, low sodium)**: Low-sodium Swiss cheese is a dairy product that can be enjoyed on a kidney-friendly diet. One slice (28g) contains approximately: **Sodium:** 54mg, **Potassium:** 26mg, and **Phosphorus:** 101mg.
- **Yogurt (Non-Dairy, Coconut)**: Coconut-based yogurt is a tasty dairy alternative. A 6-ounce serving (170g) contains approximately: **Sodium:** 15mg, **Potassium:** 17mg, and **Phosphorus:** 0mg.
- **Cream Cheese (low sodium)**: Low-sodium cream cheese can be included in a kidney-friendly diet. One tablespoon (14.5g) contains approximately: **Sodium:** 52mg, **Potassium:** 19mg, and **Phosphorus:** 15mg.
- **Milk (Non-Dairy, Rice)**: Rice milk, unsweetened, is another good non-dairy alternative. One cup (240g) contains

approximately: **Sodium:** 86mg, **Potassium:** 27mg, and **Phosphorus:** 23mg.

- **Butter (Unsalted):** Unsalted butter is a dairy product that can be used sparingly in a kidney-friendly diet. One tablespoon (14g) contains approximately: **Sodium:** 2mg, **Potassium:** 3mg, and **Phosphorus:** 3mg.

- **Venison:** Venison is a lean source of protein that's low in sodium, potassium, and phosphorus. A 3-ounce serving of cooked venison (85g) contains approximately: **Sodium:** 58mg, **Potassium:** 236mg, and **Phosphorus:** 173mg.

- **Duck Breast (portion control):** Duck breast is a flavorful protein source relatively low in sodium, potassium, and phosphorus. Three ounces of cooked duck breast (85g) contains approximately: **Sodium:** 57mg, **Potassium:** 228mg, and **Phosphorus:** 197mg.

- **Rabbit Meat:** Rabbit meat is a lean protein source low in sodium, potassium, and phosphorus. Three ounces of cooked rabbit meat (85g) contains approximately: **Sodium:** 47mg, **Potassium:** 237mg, and **Phosphorus:** 154mg.

- **Cornish Game Hen:** Cornish game hen is a type of chicken low in sodium, potassium, and phosphorus. Three ounces of roasted Cornish game hen (85g) contains approximately: **Sodium** 70mg, **Potassium:** 231mg, and **Phosphorus:** 192mg.

- **Quail:** Quail is a lean source of protein and is low in sodium, potassium, and phosphorus. Three ounces of cooked quail (85g) contains approximately: **Sodium:** 54mg, **Potassium:** 256mg, and **Phosphorus:** 205mg.

- **Cod (portion control):** Cod is a lean, white fish low in sodium, potassium, and phosphorus, making it suitable for a kidney-friendly diet. Three ounces of cooked cod (85g) contains approximately: **Sodium:** 74mg, **Potassium:** 439mg, and **Phosphorus:** 166mg.

- **Tuna (canned in water, low sodium):** Canned tuna in water is a convenient source of protein that's low in sodium, potassium, and phosphorus. Three ounces of canned tuna in water (85g) contains approximately: **Sodium:** 35mg, **Potassium:** 187mg, and **Phosphorus:** 144mg.

- **Haddock (portion control):** Haddock is another lean, white fish that's kidney-friendly. Three ounces of cooked haddock (85g) contains approximately: **Sodium:** 74mg, **Potassium:** 364mg, and **Phosphorus:** 163mg.

- **Trout (portion control):** Trout is a tasty option for those on a kidney-friendly diet. Three ounces of cooked trout (85g) contains approximately: **Sodium:** 50mg, **Potassium:** 375mg, and **Phosphorus:** 252mg.

- **Halibut (portion control):** Halibut is a white fish low in sodium, potassium, and phosphorus. Three ounces of cooked halibut (85g) contains approximately: **Sodium:** 59mg, **Potassium:** 449mg, and **Phosphorus:** 243mg.

- **Bread (White, Low Sodium):** White bread with low sodium is a safe choice for a kidney-friendly diet. One slice (25g) contains approximately: **Sodium:** 80mg, **Potassium:** 35mg, and **Phosphorus:** 20mg.

- **Muffins (Blueberry, Homemade):** Homemade blueberry muffins, when made with kidney-friendly ingredients, can be enjoyed. One medium muffin (113g) contains approximately: **Sodium:** 230mg, **Potassium:** 75mg, and **Phosphorus:** 125mg.

- **Bagel (Plain, Small):** Small plain bagels can be incorporated into a kidney-friendly diet. One small bagel (69g) contains approximately: **Sodium:** 430mg, **Potassium:** 55mg, and **Phosphorus:** 75mg.

- **Croissant (Plain):** Plain croissants are low in minerals that can harm kidneys. One medium croissant (57g) contains approximately: **Sodium:** 330mg, **Potassium:** 58mg, and **Phosphorus:** 31mg.

- **Biscuits (Homemade, Plain):** Homemade biscuits allow control over ingredients, making them a good choice. One medium biscuit (57g) contains approximately: **Sodium:** 350mg, **Potassium:** 65mg, and **Phosphorus:** 75mg.

- **Pancakes (Homemade):** Homemade pancakes can be a treat in a kidney-friendly diet. One 4-inch pancake (38g) contains approximately: **Sodium:** 260mg, **Potassium:** 70mg, and **Phosphorus:** 85mg.
- **Waffles (Frozen, Plain):** Frozen waffles, when eaten in moderation, fit into a kidney-friendly diet. One waffle (35g) contains approximately: **Sodium:** 270mg, **Potassium:** 50mg, and **Phosphorus:** 40mg.
- **Water (Plain, Filtered):** Plain, filtered water is the best choice for hydration. It has no sodium, potassium, or phosphorus. One cup (240g) contains approximately: **Sodium:** 0mg, **Potassium:** 0mg, and **Phosphorus:** 0mg.
- **Coffee (Black, Brewed):** Black coffee is an option, but be mindful of portion sizes. One cup (240g) contains approximately: **Sodium:** 5mg, **Potassium:** 116mg, and **Phosphorus:** 0mg.
- **Tea (Green, Brewed):** Green tea is a kidney-friendly beverage. One cup (240g) contains approximately: **Sodium:** 2mg, **Potassium:** 68mg, and **Phosphorus:** 0mg.
- **Juice (Apple, Unsweetened):** Unsweetened apple juice can be consumed in moderation. One cup (240g) contains approximately: **Sodium:** 10mg, **Potassium:** 250mg, and **Phosphorus:** 20mg.
- **Juice (Cranberry, Unsweetened):** Unsweetened cranberry juice is low in sodium and phosphorus. One cup (240g) contains approximately: **Sodium:** 2mg, **Potassium:** 195mg, and **Phosphorus:** 13mg.
- **Lemonade (Homemade):** Homemade lemonade allows you to control the sugar content. One cup (240g) contains approximately: **Sodium:** 5mg, **Potassium:** 49mg, and **Phosphorus:** 6mg.
- **Milk (Non-Dairy, Almond, Unsweetened):** Unsweetened almond milk is a good non-dairy alternative. One cup (240g) contains approximately: **Sodium:** 170mg, **Potassium:** 160mg, and **Phosphorus:** 24mg.

- **Smoothie (Berries, Homemade):** Homemade berry smoothies can be a tasty treat. One cup (240g) contains approximately: **Sodium:** 70mg, **Potassium:** 144mg, and **Phosphorus:** 35mg.
- **Soda (Diet, Aspartame-Sweetened):** Diet soda can be consumed occasionally. One can (355g) contains approximately: **Sodium:** 40mg, **Potassium:** 0mg, and **Phosphorus:** 0mg.
- **Hot Chocolate (Homemade, with Non-Dairy Milk):** Homemade hot chocolate made with non-dairy milk can be enjoyed in moderation. One cup (240g) contains approximately: **Sodium:** 120mg, **Potassium:** 180mg, and **Phosphorus:** 100mg.
- **Flour (White, All-Purpose):** White all-purpose flour is a versatile ingredient in baking. One cup (125g) contains approximately: **Sodium:** 2mg, **Potassium:** 100mg, and **Phosphorus:** 97mg.
- **Sugar (White, Granulated):** Granulated white sugar is often used for sweetening baked goods. One cup (200g) contains approximately: **Sodium:** 2mg, **Potassium:** 2mg, and Phosphorus: 0mg.
- **Baking Powder (Low Sodium):** Low sodium baking powder can be used for leavening. One teaspoon (5g) contains approximately: **Sodium:** 20mg, **Potassium:** 0mg, and **Phosphorus:** 15mg.
- **Baking Soda (Sodium Bicarbonate):** Baking soda is another leavening agent, but it's higher in sodium. One teaspoon (5g) contains approximately: **Sodium:** 1260mg, **Potassium:** 0mg, and **Phosphorus:** 0mg.
- **Oil (Canola):** Oil is commonly used in baking and is low in minerals. One tablespoon (14g) contains approximately: **Sodium:** 0mg, **Potassium:** 0mg, and **Phosphorus:** 0mg.
- **Egg (Whole, Raw):** Whole eggs are a staple in many baking recipes. One large egg (50g) contains approximately: **Sodium:** 70mg, **Potassium:** 69mg, and **Phosphorus:** 95mg.

- **Cocoa Powder (Unsweetened)**: Unsweetened cocoa powder can be used for making chocolate-flavored baked goods. One tablespoon (5g) contains approximately: **Sodium:** 1mg, **Potassium:** 82mg, and **Phosphorus:** 14mg.
- **Vanilla Extract (Pure)**: Pure vanilla extract is used for flavoring. One teaspoon (4g) contains approximately: **Sodium:** 1mg, **Potassium:** 12mg, and **Phosphorus:** 0mg.
- **Honey (Raw, Unfiltered)**: Raw and unfiltered honey can be used as a natural sweetener in baked goods. One tablespoon (21g) contains approximately: **Sodium:** 1mg, **Potassium:** 11mg, and **Phosphorus:** 0mg.
- **Maple Syrup (Pure)**: Pure maple syrup is another natural sweetener option for baked goods. One tablespoon (20g) contains approximately: **Sodium:** 2mg, **Potassium:** 42mg, and **Phosphorus:** 3mg.
- **Cornstarch**: Cornstarch can be used as a thickening agent in baking recipes. One tablespoon (8g) contains approximately: **Sodium:** 0mg, **Potassium:** 0mg, and **Phosphorus:** 0mg.
- **Flaxseed Meal**: Flaxseed meal is a good source of omega-3 fatty acids and can be used as an egg substitute in baking. One tablespoon (8g) contains approximately: **Sodium:** 1mg, **Potassium:** 37mg, and **Phosphorus:** 55mg.
- **Almond Flour**: Almond flour is a gluten-free alternative to all-purpose flour and is lower in minerals. One cup (92g) contains approximately: **Sodium:** 0mg, **Potassium:** 370mg, and **Phosphorus:** 629mg.
- **Coconut Flour**: Coconut flour is another gluten-free option that is also low in minerals. One cup (112g) contains approximately: **Sodium:** 16mg, **Potassium:** 412mg, and **Phosphorus:** 764mg.
- **Unsweetened Applesauce**: Unsweetened applesauce can be used as a replacement for oil or butter in baking recipes. One cup (240g) contains approximately: **Sodium:** 7mg, **Potassium:** 130mg, and **Phosphorus:** 10mg.

- **Banana (mashed, portion control):** Mashed bananas can also be used as a replacement for oil or butter in baking recipes. One medium banana (118g) contains approximately: **Sodium:** 1mg, **Potassium:** 422mg, and **Phosphorus:** 26mg.
- **Black Pepper:** Black pepper can add a spicy kick without adding sodium. One teaspoon (2g) contains approximately: **Sodium:** 1mg, **Potassium:** 37mg, and **Phosphorus:** 4mg.
- **Cinnamon (Ground):** Ground cinnamon adds a sweet and spicy flavor to your dishes. One teaspoon (2.6g) contains approximately: **Sodium:** 0mg, **Potassium:** 11mg, and **Phosphorus:** 1mg.
- **Garlic Powder:** Garlic powder offers a great way to add flavor to dishes without sodium. One teaspoon (3.1g) contains approximately: **Sodium:** 1mg, **Potassium:** 31mg, and **Phosphorus:** 5mg.
- **Onion Powder:** Onion powder is a great flavor addition and is low in minerals. One teaspoon (2.4g) contains approximately: **Sodium:** 1mg, **Potassium:** 39mg of, and **Phosphorus:** 3mg.
- **Turmeric Powder:** Turmeric powder is flavorful and can be beneficial for inflammation. One teaspoon (2.2g) contains approximately: **Sodium:** 1mg, **Potassium:** 56mg, and **Phosphorus:** 6mg.
- **Italian Seasoning:** Italian seasoning can be used in a variety of dishes. One teaspoon (1.2g) contains approximately: **Sodium:** 0mg, **Potassium:** 25mg, and **Phosphorus:** 3mg.
- **Lemon Juice (Fresh):** Fresh lemon juice adds a tangy flavor to dishes. One tablespoon (15g) contains approximately: **Sodium:** 0mg, **Potassium:** 48mg, and **Phosphorus:** 1mg.
- **Vinegar (White, Distilled):** White vinegar can add a sour kick to dishes. One tablespoon (15g) contains approximately: **Sodium:** 0mg, **Potassium:** 1mg, and **Phosphorus:** 1mg.
- **Vinegar (Balsamic):** Balsamic vinegar can be used for salads and marinades. One tablespoon (15g) contains

approximately: **Sodium:** 4mg, **Potassium:** 18mg, and **Phosphorus:** 7mg.

- <u>Chili Powder</u>: Chili powder adds a spicy kick to dishes. One teaspoon (2.7g) contains approximately: **Sodium:** 1mg, **Potassium:** 54mg, and **Phosphorus:** 7mg.
- <u>Salmon (wild-caught, portion control)</u>: Wild-caught salmon is a heart-healthy option low in sodium, potassium, and phosphorus. Three ounces of cooked wild-caught salmon (85g) contains approximately: **Sodium:** 50mg, **Potassium:** 346mg, and **Phosphorus:** 243mg.
- <u>Shrimp (portion control)</u>: Shrimp is a lean protein source low in sodium, potassium, and phosphorus. Three ounces of cooked shrimp (85g) contains approximately: **Sodium:** 166mg, **Potassium:** 40mg, and **Phosphorus:** 134mg.
- <u>Scallops (portion control)</u>: Scallops are a delicious seafood option low in sodium, potassium, and phosphorus. Three ounces of cooked scallops (85g) contain approximately: **Sodium:** 292mg, **Potassium:** 259mg, and **Phosphorus:** 125mg.

While these foods are beneficial, portion control and balance are key to a healthy, kidney-friendly diet. Always consult with a healthcare provider or dietitian before changing your diet.

The Role of These Foods in Managing Stage 3 CKD

For individuals diagnosed with stage 3 Chronic Kidney Disease (CKD), dietary habits play a significant role in maintaining kidney function and overall health. It's important to focus on foods low in potassium, like the ones listed above, as high potassium levels can lead to hyperkalemia, which is harmful to people with CKD.

Fruits such as blackberries, red cherries, strawberries, mandarin oranges, and red apples are not only low in potassium. Still, they are also packed with antioxidants and vitamins, which help to strengthen the immune system and combat inflammation. Vegetables like white mushrooms, romaine lettuce, red bell peppers, kale, and zucchini are also low in potassium and high in essential nutrients like fiber and vitamins.

Protein is another essential nutrient, and sources such as beef, chicken, shrimp, and turkey provide high-quality protein without the excess potassium. These proteins are critical for repairing body tissues and maintaining good health.

Adding herbs and spices like scallions, cilantro, and parsley can provide flavor and variety to dishes while keeping potassium content low. Healthy oils like canola and olive oil are low in potassium and provide beneficial fats, which are crucial for heart health. Consumables like black coffee, when had in moderation, can be included in a kidney-friendly diet due to their low potassium content.

It is important to remember that while these foods are beneficial, balance and portion control are key. Overconsumption of food can lead to unwanted effects and may negatively impact health. Always consult with a healthcare provider or dietitian before changing your diet. Managing CKD isn't solely about avoiding certain foods; it's about creating a balanced, nutritious eating plan that supports overall health while also being kidney friendly.

5

FOODS TO LIMIT OR AVOID

W hile focusing on foods beneficial for managing stage 3 CKD is important, certain foods and beverages should be limited or avoided altogether.

Comprehensive List of Foods that may exacerbate kidney disease for seniors on stage 3

- <u>Instant Noodles</u>: This popular quick meal is high in sodium. One serving (about 85 grams) contains roughly 1,660 milligrams of **sodium**, 300 milligrams of **potassium**, and 100 milligrams of **phosphorus.**
- <u>Pretzels:</u> A 1-ounce serving of pretzels can contain around 325 milligrams of **sodium**, 65 milligrams of **potassium**, and less than 1 milligram of **phosphorus.**
- <u>Cheese</u>: Even though it's a good source of protein, cheese can be high in sodium and phosphorus. One slice (about 28 grams) of cheddar cheese contains approximately 180 milligrams of **sodium**, 20 milligrams of **potassium**, and 145 **phosphorus.**

- **Cottage Cheese:** This is high in sodium and phosphorus. One cup (about 200 grams) contains roughly 920 milligrams of **sodium**, 132 milligrams of **potassium**, and 303 milligrams of **phosphorus.**
- **Avocados:** Although nutritious, avocados are high in **potassium.** They contain approximately 975 milligrams per cup.
- **Oranges and Orange Juice:** These are rich in **potassium**, with one orange offering around 333 milligrams and a cup of orange juice containing about 473 milligrams.
- **Cantaloupe and Honeydew Melons:** These fruits are high in **potassium**, containing around 430 milligrams per cup.
- **Prunes:** Prunes, as well as prune juice, have high levels of potassium and phosphorus. Five prunes have around 292 milligrams of **potassium** and 45 milligrams of **phosphorus**; a cup of prune juice contains about 707 and 51 milligrams of phosphorus.
- **Bananas:** Bananas are full of **potassium**, with one medium banana containing approximately 422 milligrams.
- **Tomatoes:** Tomatoes are high in potassium, especially when condensed into sauces, purees, and juice. One cup of tomato juice contains approximately 527 milligrams of **potassium.**
- **Dates, Raisins, and Figs:** These dried fruits are high in potassium. One cup of raisins contains about 1,086 milligrams of **potassium.**
- **Kiwi:** A single kiwi fruit contains about 215 milligrams of **potassium.**
- **Pomegranates:** One pomegranate holds about 666 milligrams of **potassium.**
- **Star Fruit:** This fruit is not only high in potassium, but it also has a toxic substance for people with kidney disease and should be avoided. One cup of star fruit contains about 176 milligrams of **potassium.**
- **Apricots:** Fresh apricots are a rich source of potassium. One apricot has approximately 150 milligrams of potassium.

Dried apricots have even more **potassium**, with half a cup packing about 756 milligrams.

- **Spinach**: When raw, spinach's potassium content might not seem too high (around 167 milligrams in one cup), but when cooked, its **potassium** levels skyrocket to about 839 milligrams per cup.
- **Potatoes and Sweet Potatoes:** These starchy veggies are high in **potassium**. One medium potato contains about 926 milligrams, while a medium sweet potato has about 541 milligrams.
- **Artichokes**: Artichokes are rich in **potassium**, with one medium artichoke containing about 343 milligrams.
- **Beet Greens:** Beet greens are high in potassium. One cup has around 1,309 milligrams of **potassium**, 106 milligrams of **sodium**, and 42 milligrams of **phosphorus**.
- **Okra:** This vegetable is high in potassium. A half-cup serving of sliced, cooked okra contains about 147 milligrams of **potassium**, 460 milligrams of **sodium**, and 36 milligrams of **phosphorus**.
- **Rutabagas**: A cup of cubed rutabagas has around 499 milligrams of **potassium**, 28 milligrams of **sodium**, and 74 milligrams of **phosphorus**.
- **Brussels Sprouts:** Brussels sprouts are high in potassium. One cup of cooked Brussels sprouts has about 495 milligrams of **potassium**, 16 milligrams of **sodium**, and 56 **phosphorus**.
- **Winter Squash:** This vegetable is high in potassium. One cup of baked Hubbard squash contains about 494 milligrams of **potassium**, 5 milligrams of **sodium**, and 59 milligrams of **phosphorus**.
- **Collard Greens:** Collard greens are rich in potassium. One cup of cooked collard greens contains around 177 milligrams of **potassium**, 16 milligrams of **sodium**, and 27 milligrams of **phosphorus**.
- **Green Peppers**: Green peppers have high levels of potassium. One cup of raw green pepper strips contains

around 261 milligrams of **potassium**, 3 milligrams of **sodium**, and 20 milligrams of **phosphorus**.

- <u>Bamboo Shoots</u>: One cup of cooked, sliced bamboo shoots contains around 533 milligrams of **potassium**, 1 milligram of **sodium**, and 33 **phosphorus**.
- <u>Parsley</u>: This herb is high in **potassium**, with one tablespoon containing approximately 150 milligrams.
- <u>Quinoa</u>: This grain is a good source of **potassium**, with one cup cooked providing around 317 milligrams.
- <u>Soy Products:</u> Soy products, such as tofu and tempeh, are high in potassium. Half a block of tofu contains approximately 443 milligrams of **potassium**.
- <u>Nuts</u>: Nuts, especially almonds and cashews, are high in **potassium**. One ounce of almonds contains around 200 milligrams and one ounce of cashews packs in about 187 milligrams.
- <u>Seeds</u>: Seeds, like pumpkin and sunflower seeds, are high in potassium. One ounce of pumpkin seeds has about 229 milligrams of **potassium**, and one ounce of sunflower seeds contains approximately 241 milligrams.
- <u>Milk and Milk Products:</u> These are high in phosphorus and potassium. A cup of milk has approximately 366 milligrams of **potassium** and 230 milligrams of **phosphorus**.
- <u>Sodas and Colas:</u> These can contain high levels of phosphorus. One can (355 milliliters) of cola contains about 33 milligrams of **phosphorus** and 15 milligrams of **potassium**.
- <u>Coconut Water:</u> While hydrating, this beverage is extremely high in potassium. One cup contains approximately 600 milligrams of **potassium**.
- <u>Certain Herbal Teas:</u> Some herbal teas, like those made from dandelion or nettle leaf, contain high amounts of **potassium** and should be avoided.

- **Vegetable Juices:** Some vegetable juices can be high in potassium and sodium. One cup of carrot juice, for instance, contains roughly 689 milligrams of **potassium.**
- **Alcoholic Beverages**: Alcohol can be dehydrating and affect kidney function. It also contains varying amounts of **potassium** and **phosphorus.**
- **Sports Drinks**: These drinks are often high in potassium and sodium to replace electrolytes lost during exercise. One bottle (591 milliliters) of a sports drink contains about 127 milligrams of **potassium.**
- **Bottled Water:** Some types of bottled water can be high in **sodium, potassium**, or other minerals and should be consumed cautiously. It is important to read the nutrition label before purchasing bottled water.
- **Canned Soups:** High in sodium and potassium, canned soups are not recommended for a kidney-friendly diet. One cup of canned chicken noodle soup contains around 760 milligrams of **sodium**, 468 milligrams of **potassium**, and 30 milligrams of **phosphorus.**
- **Processed Meats:** Processed meats like bacon, sausages, and deli meats are high in sodium and phosphorus. Two slices of bacon have approximately 270 milligrams of **sodium**, 150 milligrams of **potassium**, and 100 milligrams of **phosphorus.**
- **Cheese**: Cheese, particularly processed cheese, is high in sodium and phosphorus. One ounce of American cheese contains about 406 milligrams of **sodium**, 79 milligrams of **potassium**, and 145 **phosphorus.**
- **Fast Foods:** Foods like burgers, fries, and pizzas are high in sodium and phosphorus. A medium serving of fries may contain around 266 milligrams of **sodium**, 455 milligrams of **potassium**, and 57 milligrams of **phosphorus.**
- **Snack Foods:** Packaged snacks like chips, crackers, and pretzels are typically high in sodium and phosphorus. One ounce of potato chips contains approximately 149 milligrams

of **sodium**, 466 milligrams of **potassium**, and 22 milligrams of **phosphorus**.

- **Canned Vegetables**: While vegetables are generally good for you, canned vegetables can be high in sodium. One cup of canned corn, for instance, contains roughly 384 milligrams of **sodium**, 396 milligrams of **potassium**, and 55 milligrams of **phosphorus**.
- **Pickles**: These are high in sodium. One medium pickle contains around 785 milligrams of **sodium**, 125 milligrams of **potassium**, and 20 milligrams of **phosphorus**.
- **Instant Noodles:** Fast and convenient, these are unfortunately high in sodium and potassium. One packet of instant noodles contains approximately 1,166 milligrams of **sodium**, 205 milligrams of **potassium**, and 64 milligrams of **phosphorus**.
- **Baked Beans**: A staple of many diets, baked beans can be high in sodium and potassium. One cup of canned, low-sodium baked beans contains about 1,006 milligrams of **sodium**, 752 milligrams of **potassium**, and 183 milligrams of **phosphorus**.
- **Soy Sauce:** This popular condiment is high in sodium. One tablespoon of soy sauce contains roughly 879 milligrams of **sodium**, 52 milligrams of **potassium**, and 24 milligrams of **phosphorus**.
- **Aged and Smoked Meats:** These meats are high in both sodium and phosphorus. Two slices of smoked turkey contain approximately 310 milligrams of **sodium**, 350 milligrams of **potassium**, and 250 milligrams of **phosphorus**.
- **Instant Mashed Potatoes**: These are often high in sodium and potassium. One cup of instant mashed potatoes contains around 1,067 milligrams of **sodium**, 358 milligrams of **potassium**, and 131 milligrams of **phosphorus**.
- **Cured Meats**: These meats are high in sodium and phosphorus. One slice of ham contains about 1,312

milligrams of **sodium**, 140 milligrams of **potassium**, and 200 milligrams of **phosphorus**.

- <u>Sauerkraut:</u> This fermented food is typically high in sodium. One cup of sauerkraut contains roughly 939 milligrams of **sodium**, 371 milligrams of **potassium**, and 23 milligrams of **phosphorus**.
- <u>Canned Fish:</u> Canned fish can be high in sodium and sometimes contain added salt. One can (165 grams) of canned sardines contains approximately 399 milligrams of **sodium**, 296 milligrams of **potassium**, and 123 milligrams of **phosphorus**.
- <u>Beef Jerky:</u> This popular snack is high in sodium. One ounce of beef jerky contains about 506 milligrams of **sodium**, 214 milligrams of **potassium**, and 9 milligrams of **phosphorus**.
- <u>Corned Beef:</u> Typically used in sandwiches, corned beef is high in sodium and phosphorus. Three ounces of corned beef contains around 827 milligrams of **sodium**, 256 milligrams of **potassium**, and 210 milligrams of **phosphorus**.
- <u>Hot Dogs:</u> A popular fast food item, hot dogs are high in sodium and phosphorus. One hot dog contains approximately 562 milligrams of **sodium**, 148 milligrams of **potassium**, and 150 milligrams of **phosphorus**.
- <u>Cornish Game Hens</u>: These small birds are often high in sodium. One hen contains about 1,190 **sodium**, 647 milligrams of **potassium**, and 490 milligrams of **phosphorus**.
- <u>Salami:</u> This cured sausage is high in sodium. Four slices of salami contain roughly 780 milligrams of **sodium**, 176 milligrams of **potassium**, and 100 milligrams of **phosphorus**.
- <u>Pastrami</u>: Often used in sandwiches, pastrami is high in sodium. Three slices contain approximately 710 milligrams of **sodium**, 170 milligrams of **potassium**, and 75 milligrams of **phosphorus**.
- <u>Pizza Rolls</u>: These convenient snacks are high in sodium and phosphorus. One roll contains around 32 milligrams of

sodium, 30 milligrams of **potassium**, and 4 milligrams of **phosphorus**.

- <u>Salted Nuts:</u> While nuts are generally a healthy snack, salted varieties can be high in sodium. For example, one ounce of salted peanuts contains about 230 milligrams of **sodium**, 190 milligrams of **potassium**, and 100 milligrams of **phosphorus**.
- <u>Cured Cheeses:</u> These cheeses are high in sodium and phosphorus. One ounce of cured cheese can contain approximately 400-600 milligrams of **sodium**, 70-120 milligrams of **potassium**, and 90-150 milligrams of **phosphorus**, depending on the type.
- <u>Canned Soups:</u> Canned soups are often high in sodium and potassium. One cup of canned chicken noodle soup contains roughly 866 milligrams of **sodium**, 102 milligrams of **potassium**, and 63 milligrams of **phosphorus**.
- <u>Canned Tuna</u>: Tuna, especially canned ones, can be high in sodium and phosphorus. One can (165 grams) of canned tuna contains approximately 339 milligrams of **sodium**, 252 milligrams of **potassium**, and 252 milligrams of **phosphorus**.
- <u>Smoked Salmon</u>: Though delicious, smoked salmon can be quite high in sodium. Three ounces of smoked salmon contains around 666 milligrams of **sodium**, 347 milligrams of **potassium**, and 15 milligrams of **phosphorus**.
- <u>Canned Shrimp</u>: Canned shrimp, especially those preserved in brine, are high in sodium. A 3-ounce serving contains roughly 805 milligrams of **sodium**, 204 milligrams of **potassium**, and 190 milligrams of **phosphorus**.
- <u>Anchovies</u>: These small, oily fish are often high in sodium. Ten anchovy fillets contain about 1,130 milligrams of **sodium**, 147 milligrams of **potassium**, and 97 milligrams of **phosphorus**.
- <u>Clams</u>: Clams, particularly canned or smoked, can be high in sodium. Three ounces of canned clams contain approximately 697 milligrams of **sodium**, 536 milligrams of **potassium**, and 534 milligrams of **phosphorus**.

- **Store-Bought Fruit Juices:** These beverages can be high in potassium. A 250ml glass of orange juice contains approximately 475 milligrams of **potassium** and negligible amounts of **sodium** and **phosphorus**.
- **Pre-made Smoothies:** Depending on the ingredients, these can be high in potassium and phosphorus. A 250ml serving of a store-bought banana smoothie contains roughly 400 milligrams of **potassium**, 120 milligrams of **sodium**, and 115 milligrams of **phosphorus**.
- **Colas and Sodas:** These drinks are often high in phosphorus due to added phosphoric acid. A 355ml can of cola contains around 50 milligrams of **phosphorus**, 20 milligrams of **sodium**, and negligible amounts of **potassium**.
- **Sports Drinks:** These beverages are typically high in sodium and potassium. A 20-ounce serving of a sports drink contains approximately 270 milligrams of **sodium**, 75 milligrams of **potassium**, and little to no **phosphorus**.
- **Alcoholic Beverages:** Alcohol can contribute to dehydration, which can stress the kidneys. A 100ml serving of red wine contains about 7 milligrams of **sodium**, 127 milligrams of **potassium**, and 9 milligrams of **phosphorus**.
- **Coffee:** Coffee, especially when consumed in excess, can be high in potassium. A 240ml cup of black coffee contains roughly 116 milligrams of **potassium**, 5 milligrams of **sodium**, and less than 1 milligram of **phosphorus**.
- **Hot Cocoa:** Prepared with milk and cocoa powder, this drink can be high in phosphorus. A 250ml cup of hot cocoa contains about 250 milligrams of **phosphorus**, 150 milligrams of **sodium**, and 370 milligrams of **potassium**.
- **Milk:** Dairy products, including milk, are high in phosphorus. One cup (250ml) of whole milk contains approximately 230 milligrams of **phosphorus**, 105 milligrams of **sodium**, and 366 milligrams of **potassium**.
- **Tea:** Certain types of tea can be high in potassium. One cup (240ml) of black tea contains roughly 88 milligrams of

potassium, negligible amounts of **sodium**, and less than 1 milligram of **phosphorus**.

- **Chocolate Milk:** This sweet treat is high in phosphorus due to the combination of milk and chocolate. One cup (250ml) of chocolate milk contains about 300 milligrams of **phosphorus**, 200 milligrams of **sodium**, and 400 milligrams of **potassium**.

- **Energy Drinks:** These drinks often contain high levels of caffeine and added sugars, which can harm the kidneys. A 16-ounce serving of an energy drink contains roughly 140 milligrams of caffeine, 370 milligrams of **sodium**, and negligible amounts of **potassium** and **phosphorus**.

- **Bottled Iced Tea**: Similar to brewed tea, bottled versions can also be high in potassium. An 18.5-ounce bottle of iced tea contains around 160 milligrams of **potassium**, negligible amounts of **sodium**, and less than 1 milligram of **phosphorus**.

- **Fruit Punch**: This sweet beverage is high in added sugars and can harm the kidneys if consumed excessively. An 8-ounce serving contains roughly 50 grams of sugar, as well as small amounts of **sodium** and **potassium**.

- **Flavored Waters:** While marketed as a healthier alternative to sodas, flavored waters can still be high in added sugars and artificial sweeteners. A 500ml bottle contains around 12 grams of sugar, negligible amounts of **sodium**, and less than 1 milligram of **phosphorus**.

- **Beer**: Like other alcoholic beverages, beer can contribute to dehydration and stress the kidneys. One 12-ounce serving contains approximately 7 milligrams of **sodium**, 91 milligrams of **potassium**, and negligible amounts of **phosphorus**.

- **Wine Coolers**: These sweetened drinks are high in added sugars and should be consumed in moderation. A 12-ounce serving contains roughly 20 grams of sugar, as well as small amounts of **sodium** and **potassium**.

- <u>Energy Shots</u>: Similar to energy drinks, these concentrated shots can contain high levels of caffeine and added sugars. A 2-ounce serving contains approximately 200 milligrams of caffeine, 150 milligrams of **sodium**, and negligible amounts of **potassium** and **phosphorus**.
- <u>Flavored Milk Alternatives</u>: Plant-based milk alternatives, such as almond and coconut milk, can be high in phosphorus due to added fortifications. One cup (250ml) of fortified almond milk contains around 240 milligrams of **phosphorus**, 135 milligrams of **sodium**, and 170 milligrams of **potassium**.
- <u>Infused Waters:</u> While a popular trend for hydration, infused waters can be high in potassium depending on the fruits and vegetables used. A 500ml bottle of cucumber-infused water contains approximately 180 milligrams of **potassium**, negligible amounts of **sodium**, and less than 1 milligram of **phosphorus**.
- <u>Coconut Water:</u> This trendy beverage is marketed as a natural source of electrolytes, but it can be high in potassium. An 11-ounce serving contains around 500 milligrams of **potassium**, negligible amounts of **sodium**, and less than 1 milligram of **phosphorus**.
- <u>Sparkling Water</u>: While generally a healthy alternative to sugary beverages, some sparkling waters can be high in sodium. A 12-ounce can contain roughly 25 milligrams of **sodium**, as well as small amounts of **potassium** and **phosphorus**.
- <u>Fruit Smoothies</u>: Like pre-made smoothies, homemade versions can be high in potassium and phosphorus, depending on the ingredients used. A 250ml serving of a strawberry banana smoothie contains approximately 400 milligrams of **potassium**, 115 milligrams of **sodium**, and 240 milligrams of **phosphorus**.
- <u>Fruit Juice</u>: While a popular choice for breakfast, fruit juices can be high in potassium and should be consumed in

moderation. One cup (250ml) of store-bought orange juice contains around 460 milligrams of **potassium**, 5 milligrams of **sodium**, and less than 1 milligram of **phosphorus**.

- **Soy Sauce**: This is high in sodium and, thus, not recommended for a kidney-friendly diet. One tablespoon (15) contains approximately 879 milligrams of **sodium**, 37 milligrams of **potassium**, and 5 milligrams of **phosphorus**.
- **Tomato Sauce**: Due to its high potassium content, tomato sauce should be limited. A half-cup (125ml) serving contains about 405 milligrams of **potassium**, 10 milligrams of **sodium**, and 19 milligrams of **phosphorus**.
- **Prepared Mustard**: A common condiment, it can be high in sodium. One teaspoon (5ml) contains roughly 56 milligrams of **sodium**, 11 milligrams of **potassium**, and 9 milligrams of **phosphorus**.
- **Packaged Gravy Mixes:** These can be high in both sodium and phosphorus. A 1-ounce serving contains approximately 340 milligrams of **sodium**, 35 milligrams of **potassium**, and 40 milligrams of **phosphorus**.
- **Relish**: This condiment can be high in sodium and should be limited to a kidney-friendly diet. One tablespoon (15) contains about 122 milligrams of **sodium**, 12 milligrams of **potassium**, and less than 1 milligram of **phosphorus**.
- **Seasoning Mixes**: Packaged seasoning mixes can be high in sodium. One tablespoon (15ml) of a taco seasoning mix contains roughly 380 milligrams of **sodium**, 35 milligrams of **potassium**, and less than 1 milligram of **phosphorus**.
- **Barbecue Sauce**: Though a popular flavor enhancer, it's often high in sodium and potassium. Two tablespoons (30ml) contain approximately 280 milligrams of **sodium**, 140 milligrams of **potassium**, and 15 milligrams of **phosphorus**.
- **Worcestershire Sauce**: This sauce is high in sodium and should be used sparingly. One tablespoon (15) contains about 195 milligrams of **sodium**, 67 milligrams of **potassium**, and less than 1 milligram of **phosphorus**.

- **Ketchup:** A high potassium content can make this a less-than-ideal choice for a kidney-friendly diet. One tablespoon (15) contains roughly 45 milligrams of **potassium**, 125 milligrams of **sodium**, and less than 1 milligram of **phosphorus**.
- **Bouillon Cubes:** These are often high in sodium. One cube contains approximately 1,110 milligrams of **sodium**, 15 milligrams of **potassium**, and less than 1 milligram of **phosphorus**.
- **Salad Dressings:** Creamy salad dressings, such as ranch or Caesar, can be high in sodium and potassium. Two tablespoons (30ml) of ranch dressing contain roughly 280 milligrams of **sodium**, 90 milligrams of **potassium**, and less than 1 milligram of **phosphorus**.
- **Soy Products:** Soy-based foods can be high in potassium and should be limited to a kidney-friendly diet. One cup (250ml) of soy milk contains approximately 300 milligrams of **potassium**, 115 milligrams of **sodium**, and 230 milligrams of **phosphorus**.
- **Canned Soup:** A common convenience food, canned soup is typically high in sodium. One cup (250ml) contains approximately 770 milligrams of **sodium**, 200 milligrams of **potassium**, and 50 milligrams of **phosphorus**.
- **Protein Bars:** Though often marketed as a healthy snack, many protein bars contain high phosphorus levels and should be eaten sparingly. One chocolate peanut butter protein bar contains approximately 200 milligrams of **phosphorus**, 270 milligrams of **sodium**, and 200 milligrams of **potassium**.

Why these foods should be limited or avoided?

Many foods can fit into a kidney-friendly diet if they are consumed in moderation. Working with a healthcare professional or registered dietitian is important to create a meal plan that meets your unique needs and restrictions. By making small changes and being mindful of portion sizes, you can still enjoy a varied and healthy diet while managing kidney disease. Always read food labels and choose lower phosphorus, potassium, and sodium options when possible. Eating well is important for managing kidney disease and can help improve overall health and well-being. So, consult your healthcare team and make informed choices about your foods.

Certain foods should be limited or avoided by those managing kidney disease due to their high content of certain minerals, particularly potassium, phosphorus, and sodium. Though essential for the body, these elements can accumulate to harmful levels in individuals with kidney disease, as the kidneys filter excess amounts from the blood.

High potassium levels in the blood can lead to a condition called hyperkalemia, which can cause heart problems. Therefore, foods high in potassium, like bananas, oranges, potatoes, and tomatoes, should be consumed in moderation.

Similarly, phosphorus, which helps build strong bones and teeth, can be harmful when levels become too high, leading to itching, bone and joint pain, and more serious complications like heart disease. Foods such as dairy products, beans, lentils, nuts, and whole grains are high in phosphorus and should be limited.

Excess sodium can cause fluid retention and increase blood pressure, complicating kidney disease and leading to heart problems. It is found in high amounts in processed foods like canned soups, fast foods, and salted snacks.

In addition, protein is another nutrient that needs to be monitored. While essential for tissue repair and growth, protein can strain the kidneys if consumed in high amounts. It should not be completely avoided, but portion control is key.

For a kidney-friendly diet, it's crucial to remember that moderation is key, and portion sizes should be carefully managed. Always read food labels, choose lower phosphorus, potassium, and sodium options, and consider working with a healthcare professional or registered dietitian to create a meal plan that meets your unique needs. You can still enjoy a varied and healthy diet while managing kidney disease by making informed choices.

LIKE OUR BOOK? LEAVE A REVIEW!

Enjoyed reading our book? Share your thoughts in writing a review! Scan the QR code to leave your feedback and help others discover the inspiring journey within its pages. Your review matters to us!

6

EASY TO PREPARE KIDNEY-FRIENDLY RECIPES FOR SENIORS ON STAGE 3

Whether new to a kidney-friendly diet or just looking for new meal ideas, this chapter will provide easy and delicious recipes for breakfast, lunch, dinner, and snacks. These recipes are low in potassium, phosphorus, and sodium and high in nutrients that are beneficial for individuals with kidney disease.

Breakfast Recipes

1. Low-sodium Scrambled Eggs

Ingredients:

- 2 large eggs
- 2 tablespoons of milk
- 1 tablespoon of unsalted butter

Instructions:

- Beat eggs and milk together until well blended.

- Heat a non-stick skillet over medium heat and add butter.
- Pour in the egg mixture and stir gently until cooked.

Serving Size: 1 Serving (Good for 1 Person Only)

Nutritional Information per 100g Serving: Protein: 12.5g, Phosphorus: 186mg, Potassium: 138mg, Sodium: 142mg, Calories: 149kcal, Fiber: 0g

2. Blueberry Oatmeal

Ingredients:

- 1 cup water
- 1/2 cup old-fashioned oats
- 1/2 cup blueberries

Instructions:

- Bring water to a boil in a small saucepan.
- Stir in oats and reduce heat to a simmer.
- Cook oats until soft, about 20-30 minutes, stirring occasionally.
- Stir in blueberries and serve.

Serving Size: 1 Serving (Good for 1 Person Only)

Nutritional Information per 100g Serving: Protein: 3.1g , Phosphorus: 71mg , Potassium: 59mg , Sodium: 2mg, Calories: 71kcal, Fiber: 1.7g

3. Apple Cinnamon Porridge

Ingredients:

- 1/2 cup rice
- 1/2 chopped apple
- 1 teaspoon cinnamon
- 1 cup water

Instructions:

- Cook rice as per instructions on the package.
- Once cooked, add chopped apple and cinnamon. Stir well.
- Serve immediately while still warm.

Serving Size: 2 Servings (Good for 2 Persons)

Nutritional Information per 100g Serving: Protein: 2.2g, Phosphorus: 29mg, Potassium: 52mg, Sodium: 3mg, Calories: 62kcal, Fiber: 0.9g

4. Honey Wheat Toast with Almond Butter

Ingredients:

- 2 slices of honey wheat bread
- 2 tablespoons of almond butter

Instructions:

- Toast the bread to your preferred level of crispness.
- Spread the almond butter evenly over the toast.
- Serve immediately.

Serving Size: 1 Serving (Good for 1 Person Only)

Nutritional Information per 100g Serving: Protein: 5.3g, Phosphorus: 92mg, Potassium: 98mg, Sodium: 40mg, Calories: 210kcal, Fiber: 2.5g

5. Peach Yogurt Parfait

Ingredients:

- 1 cup of low-fat Greek yogurt
- 1 medium peach, diced
- 1 tablespoon of honey

Instructions:

- Layer half of the yogurt, peach, and honey in a glass or bowl.
- Repeat the layers with the remaining ingredients.
- Serve immediately.

Serving Size: 2 Servings (Good for 2 Persons)

Nutritional Information per 100g Serving: Protein: 9g, Phosphorus: 95mg, Potassium: 125mg, Sodium: 45mg, Calories: 110kcal, Fiber: 1g

6. Cream of Wheat Porridge

Ingredients:

- 1/2 cup cream of wheat
- 2 cups water
- 1 tablespoon sugar
- 1/4 teaspoon salt

Instructions:

- Bring water to a boil in a saucepan.
- Slowly whisk in cream of wheat, sugar, and salt.
- Reduce heat to low and simmer, stirring frequently, until the porridge is thick and creamy, about 2-3 minutes.
- Serve hot.

Serving Size: 3 Servings (Good for 3 Persons)

Nutritional Information per 100g Serving: Protein: 1.6g, Phosphorus: 55mg, Potassium: 49mg, Sodium: 81mg, Calories: 60kcal, Fiber: 0.3g

7. 6-Grain Hot Cereal

Ingredients:

- 1/2 cup 6-grain hot cereal mix
- 1 cup water
- A pinch of salt
- 1 tablespoon honey or brown sugar (optional)

Instructions:

- Bring water to a boil in a saucepan.
- Stir in the 6-grain hot cereal mix and salt.
- Reduce heat to low and simmer, stirring occasionally, for about 10-15 minutes or until the grains are tender and the water is absorbed.
- Sweeten with honey or brown sugar, if desired.
- Serve hot.

Serving Size: 2 Servings (Good for 2 Persons)

Nutritional Information per 100g Serving: Protein: 4.1g, Phosphorus: 80mg, Potassium: 110mg, Sodium: 35mg, Calories: 89kcal, Fiber: 1.5g

8. Apple Cranberry Walnut Salad

Ingredients:

- 2 cups mixed salad greens
- 1 apple, cored and chopped
- 1/4 cup dried cranberries
- 1/4 cup chopped walnuts
- 2 tablespoons apple cider vinegar
- 1 tablespoon olive oil
- A pinch of salt and pepper

Instructions:

- In a large bowl, combine the salad greens, chopped apple, dried cranberries, and chopped walnuts.
- In a small bowl, whisk together the apple cider vinegar, olive oil, salt, and pepper to make the dressing.
- Drizzle the dressing over the salad and toss to combine.
- Serve immediately.

Serving Size: 2 Servings (Good for 2 Persons)

Nutritional Information per 100g Serving: Protein: 1.9g, Phosphorus: 42mg, Potassium: 115mg, Sodium: 77mg, Calories: 90kcal, Fiber: 1.2g

9. Baba Ghanoush

Ingredients:

- 1 large eggplant
- 2 cloves garlic, minced
- 2 tablespoons tahini
- 1 tablespoon lemon juice
- 1 tablespoon olive oil
- Fresh parsley for garnish (optional)

Instructions:

- Preheat your oven to 375°F (190°C). Prick the eggplant all over with a fork and place it on a baking sheet.
- Roast the eggplant in the oven for about 45 minutes, or until the skin is charred and the interior is tender.
- Allow the eggplant to cool, then peel off and discard the skin.
- In a food processor, combine the roasted eggplant, minced garlic, tahini, and lemon juice. Process until smooth.

- Drizzle with olive oil and garnish with parsley, if desired. Serve with sliced cucumbers or bell peppers.

Serving Size: Approximately 4 Servings (Good for 4 Persons)

Nutritional Information per 100g Serving: Protein: 1.8g , Phosphorus: 26mg, Potassium: 76mg, Sodium: 46mg , Calories: 94kcal, Fiber: 2.4g

10. Chicken Brats

Ingredients:

- 4 chicken bratwursts
- 4 whole grain hot dog buns
- 1 onion, thinly sliced
- 1 bell pepper, thinly sliced
- 2 tablespoons olive oil
- 1 teaspoon garlic powder
- 1/2 teaspoon black pepper

Instructions:

- Preheat your grill on medium heat.
- In a sauté pan, heat olive oil over medium heat. Add the sliced onion and bell pepper and cook until they are tender and slightly caramelized.
- Season the chicken brats with garlic powder and black pepper.
- Grill the chicken brats for about 5-7 minutes on each side or until thoroughly cooked.
- Place the cooked brats in the whole grain buns and top with the sautéed onions and bell peppers.
- Serve immediately.

Serving Size: Approximately 4 Servings (Good for 4 Persons)

Nutritional Information per 100g Serving: Protein: 13g, Phosphorus: 58mg, Potassium: 210mg, Sodium: 370mg, Calories: 265kcal, Fiber: 0.6g

11. Salmon with Lemon-Dill Sauce

Ingredients:

- 4 (4 oz) salmon fillets
- 1 tablespoon olive oil
- Salt and pepper to taste
- 1 lemon, juiced
- 2 tablespoons fresh dill, chopped
- 1 tablespoon unsalted butter

Instructions:

- Preheat your oven to 400°F (200°C). Place the salmon fillets on a baking sheet lined with parchment paper.
- Brush the salmon with olive oil and season with a little salt and pepper.
- Bake the salmon in the preheated oven for about 12-15 minutes, or until the salmon flakes easily with a fork.
- While the salmon is baking, whisk together the lemon juice, chopped dill, and butter in a small saucepan over medium heat until the butter has melted and the sauce is heated through.
- Drizzle the lemon-dill sauce over the baked salmon fillets before serving.

Serving Size: 4 Servings (Good for 4 Persons)

Nutritional Information per 100g Serving: Protein: 20g, Phosphorus: 220mg, Potassium: 366mg, Sodium: 220mg, Calories: 180kcal, Fiber: 0.5g

12. Mango Avocado Salsa

Ingredients:

- 1 ripe mango, peeled and diced
- 1 ripe avocado, peeled and diced
- 1/2 red onion, finely chopped
- 1/2 cup chopped fresh cilantro
- Juice of 1 lime
- Salt to taste (optional)

Instructions:

- In a bowl, combine the diced mango, avocado, chopped red onion, and cilantro.
- Squeeze the lime juice over the mixture, and if desired, add a pinch of salt for taste.
- Mix well until all ingredients are combined.
- Serve immediately or refrigerate it for an hour before serving to let the flavors combine.

Serving Size: 6 Servings (Good for 6 Persons)

Nutritional Information per 100g Serving: Protein: 1.0g, Phosphorus: 20mg, Potassium: 200mg, Sodium: 10mg, Calories: 70kcal, Fiber: 2.0g

Lunch Recipes

1. Grilled Chicken Salad

Ingredients:

- 1 boneless, skinless chicken breast
- 2 cups of mixed greens
- 1 small cucumber, sliced

- 1/2 cup cherry tomatoes, halved
- 1 tablespoon olive oil
- 1/4 teaspoon black pepper

Instructions:

- Preheat grill or grill pan.
- Season chicken with black pepper and grill until fully cooked.
- Slice grilled chicken and place on top of mixed greens, cucumber, and cherry tomatoes.
- Drizzle with olive oil and serve.

Serving Size: Approximately 2 Servings (Good for 2 Persons)

Nutritional Information per 100g Serving: Protein: 19g, Phosphorus: 150mg, Potassium: 250mg, Sodium: 50mg, Calories: 150kcal, Fiber: 1.5g

2. Low-Sodium Lentil Soup

Ingredients:

- 1 cup lentils
- 4 cups water
- 1 small onion, chopped
- 2 cloves garlic, minced
- 1/2 teaspoon black pepper
- 1/2 teaspoon cumin

Instructions:

- Rinse lentils thoroughly and place in a large pot with water, onion, and garlic.
- Bring to a boil, then reduce heat and simmer until lentils are tender, about 45 minutes.
- Add pepper and cumin, stir well, and serve.

Serving Size: Approximately 8 Servings (Good for 8 Persons)

Nutritional Information per 100g Serving: Protein: 9g, Phosphorus: 60mg, Potassium: 290mg, Sodium: 30mg, Calories: 105kcal, Fiber: 3.5g

3. Tuna Salad Sandwich

Ingredients:

- 1 can (5 oz) low-sodium tuna, drained
- 2 tablespoons mayonnaise
- 2 slices of whole-grain bread
- Lettuce and tomato slices

Instructions:

- Mix tuna and mayonnaise in a bowl.
- Spread the tuna mixture onto one slice of bread.
- Top with lettuce and tomato slices and the second slice of bread.
- Cut in half and serve.

Serving Size: Approximately 2 Servings (Good for 2 Persons)

Nutritional Information per 100g Serving: Protein: 18mg, Phosphorus: 45mg, Potassium: 150mg, Sodium: 300mg, Calories: 190kcal, Fiber: 1.2mg

4. Quinoa Vegetable Stir Fry

Ingredients:

- 1 cup cooked quinoa
- 1/2 cup bell peppers, sliced
- 1/2 cup zucchini, diced
- 1/2 cup carrots, diced
- 1 tablespoon olive oil

Instructions:

- Heat olive oil in a skillet over medium heat.
- Add bell peppers, zucchini, and carrots. Stir fry until vegetables are tender.
- Add the cooked quinoa to the skillet and stir until well combined.
- Serve warm.

Serving Size: Approximately 4 Servings (Good for 4 Persons)

Nutritional Information per 100g Serving: Protein: 8mg, Phosphorus: 44mg, Potassium: 155mg, Sodium: 75mg, Calories: 120mg, Fiber: 1.8mg

5. Veggie-Packed Pasta Salad

Ingredients:

- 1 cup cooked pasta
- 1/2 cup cherry tomatoes, halved
- 1/2 cup cucumber, diced
- 1/4 cup red onion, thinly sliced
- 2 tablespoons olive oil
- 1 tablespoon vinegar

Instructions:

- Combine all ingredients in a bowl and toss until well mixed.
- Serve chilled or at room temperature.

Serving Size: Approximately 4 Servings (Good for 4 Persons)

Nutritional Information per 100g Serving: Protein: 5mg, Phosphorus: 21mg, Potassium: 70mg, Sodium: 20mg, Calories: 160mg, Fiber: 1.0mg

6. Apple Cranberry Walnut Salad

Ingredients:

- 2 cups mixed greens
- 1 apple, thinly sliced
- 1/2 cup dried cranberries
- 1/2 cup walnuts, chopped
- 1 tablespoon olive oil
- 1 tablespoon apple cider vinegar

Instructions:

- In a large bowl, assemble the mixed greens, apple slices, dried cranberries, and chopped walnuts.
- Drizzle the olive oil and apple cider vinegar over the top.
- Toss the salad until everything is evenly coated.
- Serve immediately or chill for up to 1 hour before serving.

Serving Size: Approximately 4 Servings (Good for 4 Persons)

Nutritional Information per 100g Serving: Protein: 3mg, Phosphorus: 20mg, Potassium: 115mg, Sodium: 10mg, Calories: 140mg, Fiber: 1.5mg

7. Broccoli, Garlic, and Rigatoni

Ingredients:

- 2 cups of rigatoni pasta
- 2 cups of broccoli florets
- 3 cloves of garlic, minced
- 1 tablespoon of olive oil
- Salt to taste (optional)
- Black pepper to taste

Instructions:

- Cook the rigatoni pasta according to package instructions. Drain and set aside.
- While the pasta is cooking, heat the olive oil in a pan over medium heat.
- Add the minced garlic to the pan and sauté until aromatic.
- Add the broccoli florets to the pan and continue to sauté until they are tender.
- Mix in the cooked rigatoni, season with salt (if using) and black pepper, and stir until well combined.
- Serve hot.

Serving Size: Approximately 4 Servings (Good for 4 Persons)

Nutritional Information per 100g Serving: Protein: 7mg, Phosphorus: 42mg, Potassium: 72mg, Sodium: 10mg, Calories: 130mg, Fiber: 2.1mg

8. Chicken Salad with Pineapple

Ingredients:

- 2 cups of cooked chicken breast, cubed
- 1 cup of fresh pineapple chunks
- 1/2 cup celery, chopped
- 1/4 cup red onion, finely diced
- 2 tablespoons mayonnaise
- Lettuce leaves for serving

Instructions:

- In a large bowl, combine the cooked chicken, pineapple chunks, celery, and red onion.
- Add the mayonnaise to the bowl and mix until all the ingredients are evenly coated.

- Serve the chicken salad on lettuce leaves for a low-carb option or with whole grain bread for a fulfilling sandwich.
- Enjoy this tasty and colorful salad chilled.

Serving Size: Approximately 4 Servings (Good for 4 Persons)

Nutritional Information per 100g Serving: Protein: 14mg, Phosphorus: 39mg, Potassium: 98mg, Sodium: 85mg, Calories: 150mg, Fiber: 1.3mg

9. Salmon with Lemon and Dill

Ingredients:

- 1 fresh salmon fillet (6 oz)
- 1/2 lemon, sliced
- 2 sprigs of fresh dill
- Olive oil
- Black pepper to taste

Instructions:

- Preheat your oven to 375 degrees Fahrenheit.
- Place the salmon fillet on a piece of aluminum foil and lightly coat with olive oil.
- Lay the sliced lemon and sprigs of dill over the salmon and season with black pepper.
- Wrap the foil around the salmon to create a sealed packet, ensuring that the juices will stay within the foil as the salmon cooks.
- Place the packet on a baking sheet and bake for 15-20 minutes until the salmon is cooked through.
- Serve hot with a side of steamed vegetables for a balanced meal.

Serving Size: Approximately 4 Servings (Good for 4 Persons)

Nutritional Information per 100g Serving: Protein: 20mg, Phosphorus: 35mg, Potassium: 200mg, Sodium: 58mg, Calories: 180mg, Fiber: 0.5mg

10. Chicken Tikka with Kachumber and Roti

Ingredients:

- 2 chicken breasts, boneless and skinless
- 1/2 cup plain yogurt
- 1 teaspoon turmeric
- 1 teaspoon cumin
- 1/2 teaspoon chili powder
- Salt to taste (optional)
- 1 cup diced cucumber
- 1 cup diced tomatoes
- 1/2 cup diced onion
- 1 tablespoon lemon juice
- 1 tablespoon olive oil
- 2 whole grain rotis

Instructions:

- Marinate the chicken breasts in a mixture of yogurt, turmeric, cumin, chili powder, and salt (if using). Leave to marinate for at least 2 hours.
- Bake the marinated chicken at 375 degrees Fahrenheit for 20-25 minutes, or until cooked through.
- While the chicken is baking, assemble the kachumber salad by combining cucumber, tomatoes, and onion. Dress with lemon juice and olive oil.
- Warm the whole grain rotis in a dry skillet or in the oven until hot.
- Serve the chicken tikka with a side of kachumber salad and a roti.

Serving Size: Approximately 6 Servings (Good for 6 Persons)

Nutritional Information per 100g Serving: Protein: 18mg, Phosphorus: 45mg, Potassium: 150mg, Sodium: 75mg, Calories: 165mg, Fiber: 1.7mg

11. Summer Stew of Courgette, Squash and Tomato

Ingredients:

- 1 courgette, sliced
- 1 yellow squash, sliced
- 2 ripe tomatoes, diced
- 1 onion, chopped
- 2 cloves of garlic, minced
- 2 tablespoons of olive oil
- Salt to taste (optional)
- Black pepper to taste

Instructions:

- Heat the olive oil in a large pan over medium heat.
- Add the chopped onion and minced garlic to the pan and sauté until the onion becomes translucent.
- Add the courgette and squash to the pan and continue to sauté for a few minutes.
- Add the diced tomatoes to the pan and season with salt (if using) and black pepper. Stir well to combine.
- Reduce the heat to low, cover the pan and let the stew simmer for about 20 minutes, or until the vegetables are tender.
- Serve hot with a side of whole grain bread or over cooked quinoa for a hearty meal.

Serving Size: Approximately 4 Servings (Good for 4 Persons)

Nutritional Information per 100g Serving: Protein: 4mg, Phosphorus: 20mg, Potassium: 70mg, Sodium: 5mg, Calories: 45mg, Fiber: 1.5mg

12. Chicken, Wild Rice, and Asparagus Soup

Ingredients:

- 1 chicken breast, boneless and skinless
- 1 cup of wild rice
- 2 cups of asparagus, cut into 1-inch pieces
- 1 onion, diced
- 2 cloves of garlic, minced
- 4 cups of low-sodium chicken broth
- Salt to taste (optional)
- Black pepper to taste

Instructions:

- Cook the wild rice according to package instructions and set aside.
- In a large pot, sauté the diced onion and minced garlic until the onion becomes translucent.
- Add the chicken breast to the pot and cook until it's no longer pink in the middle.
- Add the low-sodium chicken broth to the pot and bring it to a simmer.
- Cut the cooked chicken into bite-sized pieces and return it to the pot.
- Add the asparagus pieces to the pot and cook until they are tender.
- Stir in the cooked wild rice and season with salt (if using) and black pepper.
- Serve the soup hot for a wholesome and satisfying meal.

Serving Size: Approximately 8 Servings (Good for 8 Persons)

Nutritional Information per 100g Serving: Protein: 16mg, Phosphorus: 30mg, Potassium: 115mg, Sodium: 45mg, Calories: 110mg, Fiber: 1.2mg

Dinner Recipes

1. Baked Salmon with Lemon and Dill

Ingredients:

- 1 salmon fillet
- 1 lemon, sliced
- 1 sprig of fresh dill
- 1 tablespoon olive oil
- 1/4 teaspoon black pepper

Instructions:

- Preheat the oven to 375 degrees Fahrenheit.
- Place the salmon on a baking sheet and drizzle it with olive oil.
- Top the salmon with lemon slices and dill.
- Season with black pepper.
- Bake for 20 minutes or until the salmon is cooked through.
- Serve hot.

Serving Size: Approximately 4 Servings (Good for 4 Persons)

Nutritional Information per 100g Serving: Protein: 25mg, Phosphorus: 15mg, Potassium: 125mg, Sodium: 35mg, Calories: 206mg, Fiber: 0.3mg

2. Stuffed Bell Peppers

Ingredients:

- 2 bell peppers, halved and seeds removed

- 1/2 pound ground turkey
- 1/2 cup cooked brown rice
- 1 small onion, diced
- 1/4 teaspoon black pepper

Instructions:

- Preheat the oven to 350 degrees Fahrenheit.
- In a skillet, brown the ground turkey and onion.
- Stir in the cooked rice and black pepper.
- Stuff each bell pepper half with the turkey and rice mixture.
- Place the stuffed peppers in a baking dish and bake for 30 minutes.
- Serve hot.

Serving Size: Approximately 4 Servings (Good for 4 Persons)

Nutritional Information per 100g Serving: Protein: 14mg, Phosphorus: 50mg, Potassium: 210mg, Sodium: 40mg, Calories: 172mg, Fiber: 2.6mg

3. Vegetable Stir-Fry with Tofu

Ingredients:

- 1 cup tofu, cubed
- 1 cup broccoli florets
- 1/2 cup sliced bell peppers
- 1/2 cup sliced carrots
- 1 tablespoon olive oil
- 1/4 teaspoon black pepper

Instructions:

- Heat the olive oil in a skillet over medium heat.
- Add the tofu and stir-fry until golden brown.

- Add the vegetables and continue stir-frying until they're tender.
- Season with black pepper.
- Serve hot.

Serving Size: Approximately 6 Servings (Good for 6 Persons)

Nutritional Information per 100g Serving: Protein: 12mg, Phosphorus: 29mg, Potassium: 200mg, Sodium: 20mg, Calories: 150mg, Fiber: 2.4mg

4. Grilled Chicken with Steamed Veggies

Ingredients:

- 1 chicken breast
- 1 cup mixed vegetables (broccoli, carrots, bell peppers)
- 1 tablespoon olive oil
- 1/4 teaspoon black pepper

Instructions:

- Preheat grill or grill pan over medium heat.
- Season chicken with pepper and a drizzle of olive oil.
- Grill chicken for 6-8 minutes on each side or until fully cooked.
- Steam vegetables until they're tender-crisp.
- Serve hot with the chicken.

Serving Size: Approximately 3 Servings (Good for 3 Persons)

Nutritional Information per 100g Serving: Protein: 23mg, Phosphorus: 19mg, Potassium: 92mg, Sodium: 70mg, Calories: 165mg, Fiber: 1.1mg

5. Baked Cod with Lemon and Herbs

Ingredients:

- 1 cod fillet
- 1 lemon, sliced
- 1 tablespoon olive oil
- Fresh herbs (like parsley or dill)
- 1/4 teaspoon black pepper

Instructions:

- Preheat the oven to 375 degrees Fahrenheit.
- Place the cod on a baking sheet and drizzle with olive oil.
- Top with lemon slices and fresh herbs.
- Season with black pepper.
- Bake for 15-20 minutes or until the cod is cooked through.
- Serve hot.

Serving Size: Approximately 4 Servings (Good for 4 Persons)

Nutritional Information per 100g Serving: Protein: 24mg, Phosphorus: 21mg, Potassium: 80mg, Sodium: 50mg, Calories: 130mg, Fiber: 0.5mg

6. Renal Chicken Piccata

Ingredients:

- 2 boneless skinless chicken breasts, halved horizontally
- 1/4 cup all-purpose flour
- 1/2 lemon, juiced
- 1/2 cup low-sodium chicken broth
- 2 tablespoons capers, rinsed
- 1 tablespoon olive oil
- Fresh parsley, chopped (for garnish)

Instructions:

- Dredge the chicken cutlets in the flour, shaking off the excess.
- Heat the olive oil over medium heat in a large skillet.
- Cook the chicken cutlets until golden brown and cooked through, about 3-4 minutes on each side. Remove from the skillet and set aside.
- In the same skillet, add the lemon juice, chicken broth, and capers. Bring to a simmer.
- Return the chicken to the skillet and simmer until the sauce has thickened, about 5 minutes.
- Garnish with fresh parsley before serving.

Serving Size: Approximately 4 Servings (Good for 4 Persons)

Nutritional Information per 100g Serving: Protein: 26mg, Phosphorus: 20mg, Potassium: 98mg, Sodium: 50mg, Calories: 172mg, Fiber: 0mg

7. Kidney-Friendly Couscous Shrimp Recipe

Ingredients:

- 1 cup couscous
- 1/2 pound shrimp, peeled and deveined
- 1 bell pepper, chopped
- 1 zucchini, chopped
- 2 tablespoons olive oil
- 1 lemon, juiced
- 1/4 teaspoon black pepper

Instructions:

- Cook the couscous as per package instructions and set aside.
- Heat the olive oil in a skillet over medium heat.

- Add the shrimp and cook until they turn pink, about 2-3 minutes on each side. Remove the shrimp from the skillet and set aside.
- In the same skillet, add the bell pepper and zucchini. Cook until they're tender.
- Return the shrimp to the skillet and add the cooked couscous. Stir well to combine.
- Drizzle lemon juice over the mixture and season with black pepper.
- Serve hot.

Serving Size: Approximately 4 Servings (Good for 4 Persons)

Nutritional Information per 100g Serving: Protein: 18mg, Phosphorus: 22mg, Potassium: 120mg, Sodium: 60mg, Calories: 160mg, Fiber: 1.4mg

8. Chicken Tikka with Kachumber and Roti

Ingredients:

- 2 boneless skinless chicken breasts, cut into chunks
- 2 tablespoons tikka masala paste
- 1 cup natural yogurt
- 2 rotis
- For the Kachumber:
- 1 small cucumber, diced
- 2 tomatoes, seeded and diced
- 1/2 onion, finely sliced
- 1/2 lemon, juiced
- A handful of fresh cilantro leaves, chopped

Instructions:

- Combine the tikka masala paste and yogurt, then add the chicken chunks. Marinate for at least 2 hours.

- Preheat the grill to medium heat. Thread the chicken onto skewers and grill for 10-15 minutes, turning occasionally, until cooked through.
- While the chicken is grilling, prepare the Kachumber. Combine the cucumber, tomatoes, onion, lemon juice, and cilantro in a bowl. Mix well.
- Warm the rotis as per package instructions.
- Serve the chicken tikka skewers with the Kachumber and warm rotis.

Serving Size: Approximately 6 Servings (Good for 6 Persons)

Nutritional Information per 100g Serving: Protein: 22mg, Phosphorus: 18mg, Potassium: 95mg, Sodium: 58mg, Calories: 152mg, Fiber: 1.0mg

9. Tuna, Tomato, and Olive Pasta

Ingredients:

- 200 grams pasta of choice
- 1 can of tuna in water, drained
- 1 cup cherry tomatoes, halved
- 1/2 cup black olives, pitted and sliced
- 2 tablespoons olive oil
- 1/2 teaspoon black pepper

Instructions:

- Cook the pasta as per package instructions until al dente. Drain and set aside.
- Heat the olive oil in a skillet over medium heat.
- Add the tuna, tomatoes, and olives to the skillet. Stir-fry for a few minutes until the tomatoes are slightly softened.
- Add the cooked pasta to the skillet and toss well to combine.
- Season with black pepper and serve hot.

Serving Size: Approximately 4 Servings (Good for 4 Persons)

Nutritional Information per 100g Serving: Protein: 28mg, Phosphorus: 15mg, Potassium: 88mg, Sodium: 27mg, Calories: 180mg, Fiber: 0.8mg

10. Chicken, Wild Rice, and Asparagus Soup

Ingredients:

- 2 chicken breasts, boneless and skinless
- 1 cup wild rice
- 1 cup asparagus, chopped into 1-inch pieces
- 1 medium onion, diced
- 2 cloves garlic, minced
- 1 tablespoon olive oil
- 4 cups low-sodium chicken broth
- 1/2 teaspoon black pepper

Instructions:

- In a large pot, heat the olive oil over medium heat. Add the onion and garlic, and sauté until the onions are softened.
- Add the chicken breasts to the pot, and cook until no longer pink.
- Add the low-sodium chicken broth to the pot and bring to a simmer.
- Once the broth is simmering, add the wild rice to the pot and cook according to package instructions.
- When the rice is about 10 minutes from being done, add the asparagus to the pot and continue cooking until the rice is done and the asparagus is tender.
- Season with black pepper, then serve hot.

Serving Size: Approximately 6 Servings (Good for 6 Persons)

Nutritional Information per 100g Serving: Protein: 24mg, Phosphorus: 19mg, Potassium: 85mg, Sodium: 32mg, Calories: 158mg, Fiber: 1.2mg

11. Roasted Asparagus and Wild Mushroom Stew

Ingredients:

- 1 pound asparagus, trimmed
- 1/2 pound wild mushrooms, sliced
- 1 medium onion, diced
- 2 cloves garlic, minced
- 1 tablespoon olive oil
- 4 cups low-sodium vegetable broth
- 1/2 teaspoon blackAn error occurred during generation. Please try again or contact support if it continues. pepper

Instructions:

- Preheat the oven to 400 degrees F.
- Toss the trimmed asparagus with olive oil and place on a baking sheet. Roast for about 15 minutes, until tender.
- In a large pot, heat the olive oil over medium heat. Add the onion and garlic, and sauté until the onions are softened.
- Add the sliced wild mushrooms to the pot and cook until they start to release their juices.
- Pour in the low-sodium vegetable broth and bring to a simmer.
- Once the broth is simmering, add the roasted asparagus to the pot and continue cooking for about 10 minutes.
- Season with black pepper, then serve hot.

Serving Size: Approximately 8 Servings (Good for 8 Persons)

Nutritional Information per 100g Serving: Protein: 20mg, Phosphorus: 24mg, Potassium: 110mg, Sodium: 40mg, Calories: 90mg, Fiber: 2.5mg

12. Beef and Vegetable Kebabs

Ingredients:

- 1 pound lean beef, cut into cubes
- 1 bell pepper, cut into chunks
- 1 zucchini, cut into chunks
- 1 onion, cut into chunks
- 2 tablespoons olive oil
- 1/2 teaspoon black pepper

Instructions:

- Preheat the grill to medium heat.
- Thread the beef, bell pepper, zucchini, and onion chunks onto skewers, alternating between the beef and the different vegetables.
- Lightly brush the kebabs with olive oil, then season with black pepper.
- Grill the kebabs for 10-15 minutes, turning occasionally, until the beef is cooked to your desired level of doneness and the vegetables are tender.
- Serve hot.

Serving Size: Approximately 6 Servings (Good for 6 Persons)

Nutritional Information per 100g Serving: Protein: 26mg, Phosphorus: 20mg, Potassium: 95mg, Sodium: 50mg, Calories: 160mg, Fiber: 1.5mg

Snacks and Dessert Recipes

1. Cucumbers with Sour Cream Soup

Ingredients:

- 2 large cucumbers, peeled and finely diced
- 1/2 cup low-fat sour cream
- 2 cups low-sodium chicken broth
- 2 tablespoons fresh dill, finely chopped
- 1/2 teaspoon black pepper

Instructions:

- In a large bowl, combine the diced cucumbers, low-fat sour cream, and low-sodium chicken broth. Stir until well blended.
- Refrigerate the soup for at least 2 hours before serving, allowing the flavors to meld together.
- Before serving, garnish with the finely chopped fresh dill and season with black pepper.
- Serve chilled.

Serving Size: Approximately 4 Servings (Good for 4 Persons)

Nutritional Information per 100g Serving: Protein: 15mg, Phosphorus: 13mg, Potassium: 76mg, Sodium: 18mg, Calories: 42mg, Fiber: 0.9mg

2. Hungarian Sour Cherry Soup

Ingredients:

- 2 cups fresh or frozen sour cherries, pitted
- 4 cups low-sodium chicken broth
- 1/2 cup sour cream
- 1 tablespoon cornstarch

- 1/2 teaspoon black pepper

Instructions:

- In a large pot, bring the low-sodium chicken broth to a boil.
- Add the sour cherries to the pot and simmer until the cherries are soft, about 10-15 minutes.
- In a separate bowl, whisk together the sour cream and cornstarch until smooth.
- Gradually add the sour cream mixture to the pot, stirring constantly until the soup thickens.
- Season with black pepper, then serve hot or chilled, as preferred.

Serving Size: Approximately 6 Servings (Good for 6 Persons)

Nutritional Information per 100g Serving: Protein: 28mg, Phosphorus: 22mg, Potassium: 97mg, Sodium: 44mg, Calories: 105mg, Fiber: 1.7mg

3. Sweet 'n' Sour Meatballs

Ingredients:

- 1 pound lean ground beef
- 1/2 cup bread crumbs
- 1 egg, beaten
- 1/4 cup onion, minced
- 1 bell pepper, cut into chunks
- 1/2 cup pineapple chunks
- 1/2 cup low-sodium soy sauce
- 2 tablespoons apple cider vinegar
- 1 tablespoon brown sugar
- 1/2 teaspoon black pepper

Instructions:

- Preheat the oven to 350 degrees F.
- In a large bowl, combine the ground beef, bread crumbs, beaten egg, and minced onion. Shape the mixture into meatballs, then place on a baking sheet.
- Bake the meatballs for about 20 minutes, or until browned and cooked through.
- While the meatballs are cooking, in a large pan, combine the low-sodium soy sauce, apple cider vinegar, and brown sugar. Bring to a simmer over medium heat.
- Add the bell pepper and pineapple chunks to the pan and continue to simmer until the vegetables are tender.
- Once the meatballs are done, add them to the pan and stir to coat with the sauce.
- Season with black pepper, then serve hot.

Serving Size: Approximately 8 Servings (Good for 8 Persons)

Nutritional Information per 100g Serving: Protein: 18mg, Phosphorus: 22mg, Potassium: 88mg, Sodium: 72mg, Calories: 135mg, Fiber: 0.8mg

4. Birthday Popcorn

Ingredients:

- 6 cups popped popcorn
- 1/2 cup white chocolate chips, melted
- 1/4 cup rainbow sprinkles

Instructions:

- Place the popped popcorn in a large bowl.
- Drizzle the melted white chocolate over the popcorn, then gently stir to coat.

- While the chocolate is still wet, sprinkle the rainbow sprinkles over the popcorn.
- Allow the popcorn to cool until the chocolate hardens, then serve.

Serving Size: Approximately 12 Servings (Good for 12 Persons)

Nutritional Information per 100g Serving: Protein: 3mg, Phosphorus: 15mg, Potassium: 70mg, Sodium: 26mg, Calories: 110mg, Fiber: 1.2mg

5. Bolognese with Rice Noodles

Ingredients:

- 1/2 pound lean ground beef
- 1 carrot, finely diced
- 1 onion, finely diced
- 2 cloves garlic, minced
- 1 can (14.5 ounces) low-sodium diced tomatoes
- 2 tablespoons tomato paste
- 1/2 cup water
- 1/2 teaspoon black pepper
- 4 ounces rice noodles

Instructions:

- In a large pan, cook the ground beef over medium heat until browned. Remove from the pan and set aside.
- In the same pan, sauté the carrot, onion, and garlic until tender.
- Add the low-sodium diced tomatoes, tomato paste, and water to the pan. Stir to combine.
- Return the cooked ground beef to the pan, stir to combine, and simmer for 20 minutes.

- While the sauce is simmering, cook the rice noodles according to the package instructions.
- Drain the noodles and divide among plates. Top with the Bolognese sauce and serve hot.

Serving Size: Approximately 4 Servings (Good for 4 Persons)

Nutritional Information per 100g Serving: Protein: 14mg, Phosphorus: 20mg, Potassium: 87mg, Sodium: 58mg, Calories: 120mg, Fiber: 1.1mg

6. Cranberry Oatmeal Breakfast Cookies

Ingredients:

- 2 cups old-fashioned oats
- 1 cup flour
- 1/2 cup dried cranberries
- 1/2 cup unsweetened applesauce
- 1/4 cup light brown sugar
- 2 tablespoons honey
- 1 egg
- 1 teaspoon vanilla extract
- 1/2 teaspoon baking soda
- 1/4 teaspoon salt

Instructions:

- Preheat your oven to 350 degrees F and line a baking sheet with parchment paper.
- In a large bowl, combine the oats, flour, dried cranberries, brown sugar, baking soda, and salt.
- In another bowl, whisk together the unsweetened applesauce, honey, egg, and vanilla extract.
- Gradually add the wet ingredients to the dry ingredients, stirring until a dough forms.

- Using a spoon, drop the dough onto the prepared baking sheet, spacing the cookies about 2 inches apart.
- Bake for 12-15 minutes, or until the edges of the cookies are golden brown.
- Allow the cookies to cool on the baking sheet for 5 minutes, then transfer to a wire rack to cool completely.

Serving Size: Approximately 18 Servings (Good for 18 Persons)

Nutritional Information per 100g Serving: Protein: 3mg, Phosphorus: 29mg, Potassium: 102mg, Sodium: 47mg, Calories: 95mg, Fiber: 1.9mg

7. Sour Cream and Onion Turkey Burgers

Ingredients:

- 1 pound ground turkey
- 1/2 cup low-fat sour cream
- 1/2 cup finely chopped onion
- 1 clove garlic, minced
- 1/2 teaspoon black pepper
- Whole grain buns, for serving
- Lettuce and tomato, for garnish

Instructions:

- Preheat the grill or broiler.
- In a large bowl, combine the ground turkey, sour cream, onion, garlic, and black pepper. Mix until well combined.
- Form the mixture into patties and place on the preheated grill or under the broiler.
- Cook the burgers for about 5-6 minutes per side, until the internal temperature reaches 165 degrees F.
- Serve the burgers on whole grain buns, garnished with lettuce and tomato, if desired.

Serving Size: Approximately 6 Servings (Good for 6 Persons)

Nutritional Information per 100g Serving: Protein: 20mg, Phosphorus: 25mg, Potassium: 95mg, Sodium: 40mg, Calories: 150mg, Fiber: 0.9mg

8. Stuffed Strawberries

Ingredients:

- 1 pound fresh strawberries
- 8 ounces low-fat cream cheese, softened
- 1/4 cup confectioners' sugar
- 1 teaspoon vanilla extract

Instructions:

- Rinse the strawberries and pat dry. Cut off the tops and use a small spoon or melon baller to hollow out the insides.
- In a bowl, beat the low-fat cream cheese, confectioners' sugar, and vanilla extract until smooth and creamy.
- Spoon or pipe the cream cheese mixture into the hollowed strawberries.
- Refrigerate the stuffed strawberries for at least an hour before serving.

Serving Size: Approximately 15 Servings (Good for 15 Persons)

Nutritional Information per 100g Serving: Protein: 2mg, Phosphorus: 22mg, Potassium: 110mg, Sodium: 33mg, Calories: 89mg, Fiber: 0.7mg

9. Non-Dairy Yogurt

Ingredients:

- 4 cups unsweetened almond milk
- 2 teaspoons agar-agar flakes

- 2 tablespoons maple syrup
- 2 tablespoons non-dairy yogurt starter or probiotic powder

Instructions:

- In a saucepan, heat the almond milk until it begins to simmer.
- Sprinkle the agar-agar flakes into the milk and stir until dissolved.
- Remove the saucepan from the heat and let it cool to approximately 110 degrees F.
- Stir in the maple syrup and non-dairy yogurt starter or probiotic powder.
- Pour the mixture into clean glass jars and cover with a lid or plastic wrap.
- Place the jars in a warm location, such as inside your oven with the light on, for 8-12 hours or until the yogurt has set.
- Once set, refrigerate the yogurt for at least 2 hours before serving.

Serving Size: Approximately 10 Servings (Good for 10 Persons)

Nutritional Information per 100g Serving: Protein: 4mg, Phosphorus: 30mg, Potassium: 120mg, Sodium: 46mg, Calories: 60mg, Fiber: 1.0mg

10. Green Pea Snaps

Ingredients:

- 2 cups of fresh green peas
- 1 tablespoon of olive oil
- A pinch of sea salt
- Black pepper to taste

Instructions:

- Preheat your oven to 375 degrees F and line a baking sheet with parchment paper.
- In a bowl, toss the green peas with olive oil, sea salt, and black pepper.
- Spread the peas in a single layer on the prepared baking sheet.
- Bake for about 30-35 minutes, or until the peas are crispy and golden brown.
- Allow the Green Pea Snaps to cool before serving. They can be stored in an airtight container for up to a week.

Serving Size: Approximately 4 Servings (Good for 4 Persons)

Nutritional Information per 100g Serving: Protein: 5mg, Phosphorus: 40mg, Potassium: 150mg, Sodium: 25mg, Calories: 110mg, Fiber: 3.5mg

11. Marshmallow Popcorn Balls

Ingredients:

- 10 cups of popped popcorn
- 1 bag of mini marshmallows (10 ounces)
- 3 tablespoons of unsalted butter
- Non-stick cooking spray

Instructions:

- Spray a large mixing bowl with non-stick spray and place the popped popcorn inside.
- In a saucepan, melt the butter over medium heat.
- Add the mini marshmallows to the saucepan and stir until they are fully melted and smooth.
- Pour the melted marshmallow mixture over the popcorn in the bowl.
- Stir until all the popcorn is coated in the marshmallow mixture.
- Once the popcorn is cool enough to handle, spray your hands with non-stick spray and form the popcorn into balls. Place the balls on a piece of wax paper to cool and harden.

Serving Size: Approximately 20 Servings (Good for 20 Persons)

Nutritional Information per 100g Serving: Protein: 3mg, Phosphorus: 36mg, Potassium: 70mg, Sodium: 30mg, Calories: 130mg, Fiber: 1.2mg

12. Homemade Low-Potassium Fruit Sorbet

Ingredients:

- 2 cups of mixed berries (such as blueberries, strawberries, and raspberries)
- 1 cup of apple juice
- 1/2 cup of sugar
- 1 tablespoon of lemon juice

Instructions:

- In a blender, combine the mixed berries, apple juice, sugar, and lemon juice. Blend until smooth.

- Pour the mixture through a fine-mesh sieve into a large bowl to remove any seeds. Push the mixture through the sieve with the back of a spoon to extract as much liquid as possible.
- Pour the strained mixture into a shallow dish and place it in the freezer.
- Every 30 minutes for the next 2-3 hours, stir and scrape the mixture with a fork to break up the ice crystals.
- Once the sorbet is fully frozen, scoop it into bowls or cones to serve.

Serving Size: Approximately 8 Servings (Good for 8 Persons)

Nutritional Information per 100g Serving: Protein: 1mg, Phosphorus: 8mg, Potassium: 20mg, Sodium: 5mg, Calorie: 90mg, Fiber: 2mg

Adapting recipes to make them kidney-friendly primarily involves adjusting sodium, potassium, phosphorus, and protein levels.

Low Sodium: High sodium content can make it challenging for kidneys to maintain fluid balance, leading to high blood pressure. Therefore, you can substitute table salt with herbs, spices, vinegar, or lemon juice for flavor. Also, opt for fresh or frozen vegetables over canned ones, which often contain added salt.

Controlled Potassium: While potassium is necessary for nerve and muscle cell functioning, too much can lead to dangerous heart rhythms. Replace high-potassium fruits and vegetables like bananas, oranges, potatoes, and tomatoes with alternatives like apples, berries, green beans, and cabbage.

Reduced Phosphorus: Phosphorus buildup can cause bone and heart disorders. Avoid foods like dairy products, beans, lentils, nuts, and whole grains to control phosphorus levels.

Instead, consume a moderate number of low-phosphorus foods like rice, pasta, or some vegetables.

Moderate Protein: While protein is essential, overconsumption can burden the kidneys. Balance your diet with small portions of high-quality protein like fish, poultry, or lean meat.

Making a recipe kidney-friendly doesn't mean compromising on taste. With creativity and understanding, you can make delicious, satisfying, and health-conscious meals. By implementing these guidelines, you'll be well on your way to enjoying a diverse menu while caring for your kidney health.

7

DEBUNKING MYTHS ABOUT KIDNEY HEALTH DIETS

W hen it comes to maintaining kidney health, plenty of information and advice often leads to confusion and misconceptions. This chapter will debunk some common myths about kidney health diets.

Common misconceptions about what you can and cannot eat and evidence-based information to debunk these myths

Myth 1: You Should Avoid Protein Completely

While overconsumption of protein can strain the kidneys, it doesn't mean you should avoid it entirely. Protein is an essential nutrient for bodily functions. Consuming moderate amounts of high-quality protein like fish, poultry, or lean meat is key.

Myth 2: All Fruits and Vegetables are Good for Kidney Health

While fruits and vegetables contribute to overall health, some high-potassium fruits and vegetables like bananas, oranges, potatoes, and tomatoes can lead to dangerous heart rhythms in people with kidney issues, reason why they are to be limited or avoided. Opting for alternatives like apples, berries, green beans, and cabbage is essential.

Myth 3: A High Salt Diet Doesn't Affect Kidneys

High sodium content can make it challenging for kidneys to maintain fluid balance, leading to high blood pressure. It's recommended to substitute table salt with herbs, spices, vinegar, or lemon juice for flavor.

Myth 4: Drinking Excessive Water Enhances Kidney Function

While staying hydrated is crucial, excessive water consumption doesn't necessarily improve kidney function. Drinking an adequate amount of water is essential, but unnecessary overconsumption could strain the kidneys.

Myth 5: You Should Strictly Follow a Low-Carb Diet

While it's true that controlling blood sugar can help manage kidney health, not all carbohydrates are harmful. It's important to focus on consuming complex carbs, like whole grains, which are processed more slowly and stabilize blood sugar levels.

Myth 6: Avoid Dairy Products at All Costs

Phosphorus found in dairy can cause issues in people with kidney disease. However, not all dairy products are high in phosphorus. For example, cream cheese and ricotta have lower phosphorus levels and can be included in a kidney health diet in moderation.

Myth 7: All Beans Should Be Avoided

While some beans are high in potassium and phosphorus, soaking beans in water can reduce these levels. Therefore, they can still be included in a diet for kidney health if prepared properly.

Myth 8: Alcoholic Beverages are Always Harmful for Kidneys

Excessive alcohol consumption can indeed damage your kidneys. However, moderate consumption (up to one drink daily for women and two for men) is generally considered safe.

Myth 9: Artificial Sweeteners are Safer than Sugar for Kidneys

Artificial sweeteners are not necessarily safer for kidneys than sugar. Some research suggests that they pose risks to kidney health. It's best to limit both added sugars and artificial sweeteners.

Myth 10: A Vegetarian Diet Can't Provide Enough Protein for Kidney Patients

A balanced vegetarian diet can provide adequate protein for kidney patients. Foods like quinoa, soy products, and lentils are all high-quality protein sources suitable for a kidney health diet. However, monitoring the consumption of high-potassium and high-phosphorus plant foods is essential.

Understanding these myths and facts about kidney health diets can help individuals make informed decisions about their nutritional needs and preferences. Always consult a healthcare provider or a dietitian for personalized advice.

8

UNDERSTANDING SUPPLEMENTS AND MEDICATIONS

While a kidney-friendly diet is crucial for maintaining good kidney health, certain medications and supplements can also play a key role. This chapter will explore the different types of supplements and medications commonly used for kidney care.

An Overview of Useful Supplements for Kidney Health

Supplements can be a valuable addition to a kidney-friendly diet, providing essential nutrients that may not be readily available or adequately absorbed from food. However, it's critical to remember that these are not a substitute for a balanced diet or prescribed medication but should be used as a supportive measure under the guidance of a healthcare provider.

Vitamin D is one of the most crucial supplements for kidney health. The kidneys convert vitamin D into its active form, which helps regulate calcium and phosphorous levels, promoting bone health. However, damaged kidneys are often less efficient at this conversion, making supplementation beneficial.

Omega-3 fatty acids, particularly EPA and DHA, are known for their anti-inflammatory properties. They may help reduce inflammation in the kidneys, potentially slowing the progression of kidney disease. The primary source of Omega-3s is fatty fish, but supplementation could be a useful alternative for those who do not consume fish.

Another essential supplement is **B-Vitamins,** specifically B6, B12, and Folic Acid. They are known to help reduce homocysteine levels in the blood, high levels of which have been linked with heart disease and kidney damage.

Iron is typically recommended for individuals with kidney disease as they often suffer from anemia. In this condition, the body lacks enough healthy red blood cells to carry adequate oxygen to the body's tissues. Iron helps produce more red blood cells, alleviating anemia.

Probiotics are beneficial bacteria that aid digestion, reduce inflammation, and help manage urea levels, a waste product often elevated in individuals with kidney disease.

Lastly, **Coenzyme Q10 (CoQ10),** a potent antioxidant, may help manage kidney health by reducing oxidative damage. The body naturally produces CoQ10, but the production may decline with age or due to certain health conditions, making supplementation beneficial.

While these supplements may support kidney health, consulting with a healthcare provider before starting any new regimen is essential. They can provide personalized advice based on your health condition and needs.

Remember, the goal is to support kidney function and overall wellness, and each individual's requirements will vary. Responsible and informed use of supplements, paired with a kidney-friendly diet, can contribute significantly to this goal.

By understanding these supplements and how they interact with kidney health, you are actively managing your health.

Through informed decisions, you pave the way for a healthier lifestyle and better kidney health.

Interactions of Medications with Food and their Effects on Kidney Health

Medications are often an integral part of managing kidney disease, but it's essential to understand that they can interact with certain foods, impacting their effectiveness and potentially affecting kidney health.

Some of the most common medications prescribed for kidney disease are **ACE inhibitors** and **ARBs.** These medications help control blood pressure and reduce proteinuria. However, they can interact with high-potassium foods, leading to hyperkalemia, a potentially life-threatening condition. Therefore, patients taking these medications should monitor their intake of high-potassium foods like bananas, oranges, potatoes, and tomatoes.

Another class of medication frequently used is **phosphate binders.** These bind to dietary phosphorus in the gut and prevent its absorption. Since they interact directly with food, taking them with meals is crucial. High-phosphorus foods like dairy products, beans, and nuts should be moderated on these medications.

Diuretics, often known as water pills, remove excess fluid from the body. They can interact with various foods and other medications, affecting their efficacy. Certain diuretics can cause the body to lose potassium, so a healthcare provider may recommend eating more potassium-rich foods. However, other diuretics may cause the body to retain potassium, in which case a low-potassium diet would be beneficial.

Calcium channel blockers are another type of blood pressure medication that can interact with grapefruit and grapefruit juice. The fruit can increase the amount of medication in the bloodstream, amplifying side effects and potentially harming the kidneys.

Lastly, **Non-Steroidal Anti-Inflammatory Drugs (NSAIDs)**, such as ibuprofen, can harm the kidneys, particularly if taken regularly over a long period. While they don't interact with food, they should be used cautiously in patients with kidney disease.

In conclusion, patients with kidney disease need to know how their medications may interact with their diet. This information is not intended to substitute professional medical advice but to serve as a guide to prompt discussions with healthcare providers about prescription medications, potential food interactions, and their impact on kidney health. Always remember informed decisions are the cornerstone of managing any health condition effectively and successfully.

9

LIFESTYLE FACTORS THAT INFLUENCE KIDNEY HEALTH

While diet and medication are significant in managing kidney health, lifestyle factors also profoundly impact. Individuals can improve their overall well-being and support their kidneys by positively changing their habits.

Exercise, Rest, and Stress Management: The Pillars of Kidney Health

Physical activity, adequate rest, and effective stress management are crucial in supporting kidney health. Together, these three factors create a triad that can significantly influence your overall well-being and the function of your kidneys.

Exercise promotes overall health, but its kidney benefits are especially noteworthy. Regular physical activity helps control blood pressure and blood sugar levels, essential for maintaining healthy kidneys. Exercise also aids in weight management, reducing the risk of obesity, a significant risk factor for kidney disease. Activities like brisk walking, cycling, swimming, or yoga can improve kidney health.

The importance of **rest** cannot be overstated regarding kidney health. When you rest, your body repairs itself, including your kidneys. Adequate sleep each night is crucial. During this time, your body regulates blood pressure and repairs kidney tissues. Lack of sleep or disrupted sleep can lead to high blood pressure and kidney disease. Therefore, establishing a regular sleep schedule and a calming bedtime routine can significantly support kidney health.

Stress management is another key aspect of maintaining kidney health. Chronic stress can raise blood pressure and cortisol levels, harming the kidneys over time. Implementing stress management techniques into your daily routine, like mindfulness, meditation, deep breathing exercises, or engaging in hobbies, can help regulate your body's response to stress.

In conclusion, the combination of regular exercise, adequate rest, and proper stress management can profoundly impact your kidney health. Making positive changes in these areas is an empowering step towards healthier kidneys and overall well-being. Remember, the goal is consistent and mindful lifestyle changes, not an overnight transformation. Informed decisions and active steps towards a healthy lifestyle will benefit your kidneys and improve your quality of life.

10

NAVIGATING DINING OUT AND SOCIAL EVENTS

E ating out and attending social events can be challenging to maintain a healthy lifestyle, but it's not impossible. With some planning and preparation, you can enjoy these occasions without compromising your kidney health.

Navigating dining out and social events while maintaining a kidney-friendly diet doesn't have to be a daunting task. It merely requires some foresight, awareness, and a few smart strategies.

Preparation is Key

Before heading out, spend a moment researching the restaurant or the event's dining options. Many restaurants nowadays provide their menus online, allowing you to plan your meal. Look for dishes that align with your kidney-friendly diet, such as lean proteins, fresh fruits, and veggies, while avoiding high sodium or high potassium meals.

Communicate Your Dietary Requirements

Feel free to communicate your dietary needs to the waiter or chef. Most establishments are willing to accommodate special dietary requests, like preparing dishes with less salt or avoiding certain ingredients.

Portion Control

Portion control plays a crucial role in managing a healthy diet. Even kidney-friendly foods can become problematic in large quantities. Be mindful of serving sizes and consider boxing up half your meal for later.

Substitutions are Your Friend

Substitutions make a dish more suitable for your dietary needs. Swap out foods high in sodium or potassium with suitably healthy options. For instance, opt for a side salad or steamed vegetables instead of French fries.

Beverage Choices

When it comes to beverages, water is the best choice. Avoid drinks high in sugar, like sodas, caffeine, coffee, or tea.

Handling Social Events

Social events can be slightly more unpredictable than restaurants, but you can still stick to your diet. Try eating a small, kidney-friendly meal at home before attending the event. This way, you won't be starving and are less likely to overindulge in foods that may not be kidney friendly. At the event, fill your plate with fresh fruits, vegetables, and lean proteins, if available.

Remember, maintaining a kidney-friendly diet when dining out or attending social events is entirely possible with some preparation, clear communication, and wise choices. Don't let dietary restrictions prevent you from enjoying these social aspects.

By adopting these strategies and maintaining a proactive approach, you can ensure your diet supports your kidney health without compromising the enjoyment of dining out and attending social events.

Explaining Dietary Needs to Others

Sharing your dietary needs with others can often feel like a sensitive topic. However, effective communication about your kidney health requirements is essential, particularly in social settings. Here are some tips to help you address this with ease.

Be Open and Direct

Honesty is the best policy. Politely and straightforwardly, let the host know about your dietary restrictions. Explain that you're following a diet for kidney health, requiring you to limit or avoid certain foods.

Provide Information

Often, people are more than willing to accommodate dietary needs if they understand them. Briefly explain what a kidney-friendly diet entail. For instance, you might say, "I need to limit foods high in sodium, potassium, and phosphorus to keep my kidneys healthy. This includes certain meats, dairy products, and processed foods."

Offer to Bring a Dish

To help alleviate any inconvenience, offer to bring a kidney-friendly dish to share. This way, you'll know there is something you can eat, and it provides an opportunity for others to try and understand your diet.

Use Humor

When explaining your dietary needs, humor is a great way to lighten the mood. A lighthearted approach can ease potential tension and make the conversation more comfortable for both parties.

Be Gracious

Thank your host or server for their understanding and accommodation. Show appreciation for their effort to meet your dietary needs, which will likely encourage them to continue being supportive. Remember, the goal is to ensure you can stick to your dietary plan and foster understanding and empathy among your social circles.

Navigating social events with dietary restrictions doesn't have to be stressful. You can enjoy social gatherings while maintaining kidney health by openly communicating your needs, providing necessary information, and showing appreciation. This is a journey, and every step taken, meal eaten, and conversation brought you closer to achieving your goal of improved kidney health while enjoying the fullness of life.

KEEPING ON TRACK: MONITORING PROGRESS AND STAYING MOTIVATED

M aintaining a healthy lifestyle and following a kidney-friendly diet is an ongoing process. It's essential to track your progress and stay motivated along the way.

Importance of Regular Health Checks and Tracking Progress

Regular health checks are paramount in managing kidney health. These checks provide an up-to-date snapshot of your overall health and how your kidneys function. Regular medical examinations allow for early detection of any changes or potential complications related to your kidneys, ensuring timely intervention and treatment.

Blood tests, urine tests, and blood pressure readings are typically involved in these checks. Blood tests measure the amount of waste products, like creatinine and urea, in your blood, giving insight into your kidneys' filtering efficiency. Urine tests detect abnormalities that may signal kidney damage, like the presence of albumin. Regular blood pressure readings are critical, too, as high blood pressure is a common cause of kidney disease.

However, health management extends beyond these clinical checks. Self-monitoring plays a crucial role in keeping on track with your kidney-friendly lifestyle. This involves tracking your dietary intake, monitoring your blood pressure at home, weighing yourself regularly, and noting any unusual symptoms.

Keeping a healthy diary can be a helpful tool for this. Record your meals, physical activities, blood pressure readings, and weight. This tracking enables you to observe patterns and trends over time and promotes accountability, enhancing your commitment to your kidney-friendly lifestyle.

In terms of motivation, celebrate milestones, no matter how small they may seem. You may have successfully adhered to your kidney-friendly diet for a week or exercised consistently. Recognizing these achievements can provide a much-needed boost to your motivation levels.

Sharing your journey with others can also foster motivation. Join a support group or connect with others adopting a kidney-friendly lifestyle. Their experiences, insights, and encouragement can prove invaluable in maintaining your motivation.

Remember, every step you take in monitoring your health, every piece of data you track, brings you closer to achieving improved kidney health. It's not just about the destination but the journey. Embrace the process, honor your progress, and remember - your commitment to your health is your best investment ever.

Motivational Tips and Strategies to Stick with Dietary Changes

Adopting a new diet, particularly for health reasons, can be challenging. However, it can be an enriching and rewarding experience with the right mindset and strategic planning. Below are some motivational tips and strategies to help you stick with your dietary changes and make a lasting impact on your kidney health.

1. Set Realistic Goals

When embarking on a dietary change, setting attainable goals is crucial. Break your objective into smaller, manageable tasks if it seems too overwhelming. For example, instead of aiming to overhaul your entire diet immediately, start by reducing your sodium intake for the first week, then focus on potassium the next week, and so on. This incremental approach makes the task less daunting and keeps you motivated as you begin to see improvements in your health.

2. Meal Planning

Planning your meals early eliminates the stress of last-minute decisions and helps you stick to your kidney-friendly diet. Include a variety of foods you enjoy and meet your dietary requirements. Keep in mind that a healthy diet doesn't have to be boring. Experiment with different recipes and flavors to keep your meals interesting and enjoyable.

3. Positive Affirmations

Remind yourself of the reasons behind your dietary change. Write down positive affirmations and read them daily. Phrases like "I am committed to improving my kidney health" and "I am making choices that benefit my overall health" can reinforce your commitment and motivate you.

4. Reward Yourself

Celebrate your successes along the way. When you reach a milestone, reward yourself with a non-food treat, a massage, a new book, or an extra hour of relaxation. This not only keeps things exciting but also reinforces positive behavior.

5. Seek Support

Share your journey with others. Whether it's family, friends, or a support group, having a supportive community can encourage and motivate you. Regular check-ins and shared experiences can inspire you, helping you adhere to your dietary changes.

Remember, change takes time, patience, and persistence. Each decision you make brings you one step closer to improved kidney health. Embrace the journey, celebrate your progress, and stay motivated. Your commitment to your health is an investment in your future and a testament to your strength and resilience.

LIKE OUR BOOK? LEAVE A REVIEW!

Enjoyed reading our book? Share your thoughts in writing a review! Scan the QR code to leave your feedback and help others discover the inspiring journey within its pages. Your review matters to us!

CONCLUSION: THE JOURNEY TOWARDS IMPROVED KIDNEY HEALTH

The journey towards improved kidney health is a comprehensive process, not a solitary event. Throughout this book, we have delved into numerous aspects of kidney health, each crucial to establishing and maintaining your well-being. We started by understanding the essential role the kidneys play in our bodies and the impact of kidney diseases. In our quest to manage and improve kidney health, we learned the significance of regular health checks and the value of self-monitoring, emphasizing the need to be proactive and vigilant in our health journey.

We also explored the world of dietary modifications and how a kidney-friendly diet can dramatically enhance kidney function. From setting realistic goals meal planning, to maintaining a positive mindset, we discovered different strategies to ensure adherence to these changes and make them a sustainable part of our lifestyles.

As we conclude this insightful journey, remember that each step you take, and your change brings you closer to improved kidney health. It's about embracing the process, celebrating your progress, and remaining consistent. This journey may be challenging, but the rewards are well worth it.

Encouragement for Readers: Continuing the Journey Towards Better Kidney Health

As we have journeyed through the pages of this book together, we have encountered numerous strategies and actionable steps designed to enhance your kidney health. It is vital to remember that maintaining kidney health is not a one-time task but an ongoing commitment that requires determination, persistence, and positivity.

The journey to improved kidney health is unique for everyone, just like our kidneys are unique to us. It's essential to embrace this journey fully, recognizing both the challenges and the victories, and understanding that every effort you make towards healthier kidneys is a testament to your resilience and strength.

Each dietary modification, every health check, and even the smallest lifestyle changes accumulate to produce a significant impact. You've learned how to align your diet with your kidney health, monitor your health effectively, and set realistic and manageable health goals — all of these are powerful tools in your arsenal.

But remember, this book is not an endpoint; it's a launchpad – a catalyst to inspire and equip you with knowledge and strategies to continue your journey toward better kidney health. It's a comprehensive resource you can refer to, a constant companion in your journey to improved health and well-being.

Lastly, always remember that you are not alone in this journey. The kidney health community is filled with individuals who, like you, are committed to improving their health. Lean on this community for Support, share your experiences, and gain strength from their stories. Much like yours, their journey is a beacon of hope and a testament to the power of determination and resilience.

Final Thoughts on the Positive Impact of a Kidney-Friendly Diet on Overall Wellbeing

As we wrap up this enlightening narrative, it's important to underscore the profound impact a kidney-friendly diet can have on your overall well-being. This diet, rife with carefully selected foods, contributes to improved kidney function and synergistically enhances your overall health. This understanding is akin to discovering a key that unlocks a gateway to a healthier, more vibrant life.

A kidney-friendly diet is much more than a prescriptive list of do's and don'ts. It's a guide towards a sustainable lifestyle that, when embraced fully, can lead to transformative health benefits. Crucial amongst these benefits is the prevention of kidney damage and slowing the progression of kidney disease. By regulating the intake of certain nutrients, such as sodium, potassium, and phosphorus, this diet focuses on diminishing the kidneys' load, allowing them to function more efficiently.

However, the benefits of a kidney-friendly diet extend beyond the kidneys. By promoting heart-healthy choices, it contributes to cardiovascular health. This diet advocates for lean proteins, whole grains, fruits, and vegetables, all of which supply essential nutrients to your body, boost your immunity, and enhance your energy levels. It also encourages portion control and mindful eating, habits that can foster a healthier relationship with food and help maintain a balanced weight.

In essence, a kidney-friendly diet is a holistic approach to wellbeing. It recognizes that our body is a complex interplay of various systems, and caring for one aspect can positively influence others. This understanding underscores the diet's role as a powerful tool in your health arsenal, fortifying you against numerous ailments and paving the path towards a healthier life.

Remember, adopting a kidney-friendly diet is not merely a dietary change; it's a lifestyle commitment. It's a journey of learning, under-standing, and making informed choices. Throughout this journey, you'll not only take significant strides in enhancing your kidney health but also bring about a positive transformation in your overall well-being.

So, as we conclude, let's celebrate this newfound understanding and its potential to transform your health. Imbued with this knowledge, you can make informed dietary choices that enrich your health, empowering you toward a healthier, more fulfilled life. Embrace this journey with an open heart and a curious mind and watch as it unfolds a world of wellness for you.

Made in United States
Troutdale, OR
02/16/2024

17711723R00105